HE
8700.8
R 43

Reel, Adolph Frank.

The networks

DATE DUE

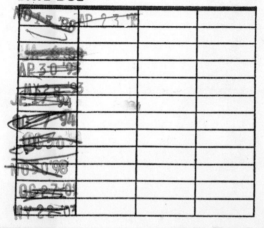

HE
8700.8
R 43

Reel, Adolph Frank.

The networks

THE NETWORKS

THE
NETWORKS

HOW THEY STOLE THE SHOW

A. Frank Reel

CHARLES SCRIBNER'S SONS / *New York*

Library of Congress Cataloging in Publication Data

Reel, Adolph Frank.
  The networks: how they stole the show.

  Includes index.
  1. Television broadcasting—United States. I. Title.
HE8700.8.R43   384.55′4′0973   79–16849
ISBN 0-684-16167-2

Grateful acknowledgment is made to quote from the following copyrighted material:
from *The View from Highway 1,* by Michael J. Arlen, copyright © 1974, 1975, 1976
Michael J. Arlen. This material appeared originally in *The New Yorker.* Reprinted by
permission of Farrar, Straus & Giroux, Inc.; from "The Observer," by Russell Baker,
copyright © 1978 The New York Times Company, reprinted by permission; from
"Living with Television: The Violence Profile," by George Gerbner and Larry P.
Gross, *Journal of Communication,* Spring 1976, copyright © 1976 The Annenberg
School of Communication, reprinted by permission; from "The Men Who Run TV
Aren't That Stupid ... They Know Us Better Than You Think," by Paul Klein, copy-
right © 1971 the NYM Corporation, reprinted by permission of *New York* Magazine.

To Virginia

CONTENTS

Introduction   ix

1. All for One and Three for All   1

2. The Making of the Monopoly   18

3. Ratings: The "Lifeblood"   31

4. The Networks and the Television Stations   42

5. The Networks and the Producers   67

6. The Networks and the News   87

7. Censorship: Public or Private?   105

8. The Networks' Invasion of Neighboring
    Domains   120

9. What Can Be Done Within the System   134

10. Alternative Sources: Cable, Pay TV, and
    Public TV   148

11. The Roads to Relief: The FCC, Congress,
    and the Courts   163

12. Which Way? Gadgetry or Government?   191

INDEX   197

Introduction

"The question of monopoly must be squarely met. It is . . . inconceivable that the American people will allow this newborn system of communication [radio] to fall exclusively into the power of any individual group or combination. . . . It cannot be thought that any single person or group shall ever have the right to determine what communication shall be made to the American people."
— *Herbert Hoover, as secretary of commerce, in an address to Congress, 1924*

A few years ago, the foreign rights representative for a Hollywood television producer described to me what he called a "typical" sales trip through Latin America. Television is a government monopoly in Latin America. For one reason or another, those Latin American officials who make the decisions about what their countrymen will watch seem to be particularly receptive to the American "action-adventure" show. It was that kind of show (an exemplary episode had been dubbed into Spanish) that the salesman tried to sell on his "typical" trip.

In one country the salesman spent hours fencing with bureaucrats, and then found that he had to get the approval of the president in order to make the sale.

I asked if the president took an extraordinary interest in cultural matters.

"I never saw him," the salesman said. "I dealt with the man who was chairman of the national television commission. We watched the show on a television screen and the president watched it on a closed-circuit monitor in the *palacio*. The chairman said the president watched every show offered for sale. I came back the next day, after the president had slept on it, and talked terms."

"The president liked the show?"

"Sure. But he preferred the terms, which included a kick-back of the purchase price. He didn't watch TV for nothing."

Although the politics of American television do not normally entail bribery, we do have a situation where what appears on our television screens can be controlled by one of three men (depending on which channel we are watching), and, like the decisions of the Latin American president, his are made on the basis of financial benefit to himself and to his corporation.

The lords of the television business, who are in a favorable position to promulgate their message, miss few opportunities to tell us that their industry is a fine example of American free enterprise. "Free enterprise" in this case is a euphemism for what is the most powerful, most effective, and most impregnable monopoly in the history of the United States: the television-network monopoly. The fact that the monster has three heads—NBC, CBS, and ABC—makes television competitive only within the most limited of terms; the three heads snap and bite at each other while fighting for an identical, virtually agreed-upon audience.

There is nothing in American financial history to compare with the success of the networks. Television is a business on which advertisers spend $6 billion a year, a business in which two-thirds of the net income goes to the three networks. The networks have shown handsome profits since the early 1950s, but their advances over recent years have been extraordinary. To put it in perspective, pretax profits accruing to all businesses increased at an average annual rate of 12 percent between 1960 and 1974, while the pretax profits of NBC, CBS, and ABC taken together went from $33.6 million to $225 million during the same period, an average annual increase of 38 percent. By 1977 the pretax profit figure had reached $555 million, more than twice that of 1974.

The financial success of the network monopoly would be of small concern if the system brought us television programming that addressed our pluralistic society in significant and imaginative ways. Those of us who grew up before the arrival of television may tend to think of it as just another means of communication, as the successor to the telegraph, telephone, wireless, and radio. By the same token, our grandparents saw the advent of the automobile as just another means of transportation, as no more than a "horseless carriage." We now know that the automobile revolutionized our economy, our landscape, our social rituals. In much the same way, television has wrought an upheaval in our culture and daily life of which we are only beginning to become aware.

Sixty million television sets are on for an average of 6 hours a day, 365 days a year. Adults spend approximately 28 percent of their leisure time watching television. Preschool children watch television for approximately one-fifth of the day, and by the time a child reaches school he will have watched the tube for more hours than he will ever spend in college classrooms. By the time he is eighteen, the child will have devoted one-sixth of his life to TV viewing. Millions of housewives do their cleaning and ironing while watching soap operas. Teen-agers do their homework with early prime-time programs providing a background, and they often sit up much of the rest of the night watching late movies.

Much of the criticism of television arises out of the feeling that what is harmless in small doses may be fatal as a steady diet. America's infatuation with television has led some observers to conclude that it has made us a country of passive watchers rather than readers. We grunt rather than talk. We absorb indiscriminately rather than think. But the most common complaint is that television is turning us into a nation of criminals and victims of criminals. A link between the alarming increase in the incidence of violent crime and the prevalence of violence in television programs has been the subject of many psychological studies and governmental investigations, of countless speeches, dissertations, and publications by doctors, congressmen, criminologists, child behaviorists, and sociologists of every description.

Network spokesmen frequently reply to criticisms of television violence by pointing rather high-mindedly to ancient Greek or Elizabethan drama, in which violence often plays a fundamental part. Violence, they say, is identical with "conflict," and without conflict there is no drama, though of course violence is only one way of dramatizing conflict. Network apologists argue further that children during the first two decades of the century were punished for reading shocking dime novels, which were supplanted in the 1930s by action comic books and gangster movies (both of which became the subject of innocuous industry "production codes"), all popular forms of entertainment for which it is impossible to prove "harmful effects."

Those who so defend television violence assume that watching the tube is similar to spending furtive hours with dime novels, hastily devouring comic books, or attending the Saturday movie matinee. As George Gerbner and Larry Gross of the Annenberg School of Communications at the University of Pennsylvania have shown, television's terms are quite different from a novel's or movie's. Writing in the *Journal of Communication* (Spring 1976), they dramatize the issue by addressing an imaginary reader born before 1950. "Could you as a 12 year old have contemplated spending an average of 6 hours *a day* at the local movie house? Not only would most parents not have permitted such behavior but most children would not have imagined the possibility. Yet, in our sample of children, nearly half the 12 year olds watch at least 6 hours of television every day."

A few years ago a newly appointed chairman of the Federal Communications Commission created a minor sensation when he advised a convention of broadcasters to spend some time watching the programs they were sending into homes. He said they would see a "vast wasteland."

There were then, as there are now, millions of people in this country who liked what television provided. Television not only affords an escape from the humdrum quality of people's lives, but it does so within a framework of reality. Television is a way of absorbing information, of staying up-to-date, of feeling a part of some larger community. Television proposes to instruct us through news programs about what is really happening in the world. And its aura of journalistic truth carries over into the realm of fiction, so that the characters in a crime show or a soap opera become as believable, as substantial, as the friendly anchorman. Although television does not encourage that distinctions be made between fiction and reality, it is nevertheless true that its most avid viewers depend upon it as a kind of ongoing story about who we are, how we live, what we are going to do next.

Over the years, apologists for commercial television have boasted of its "great moments," its "stunning breakthroughs," its "magnificent achievements." But these moments have been distinguished precisely because they are moments and break-throughs—that is, they are not the norm. For television's one primary feature is its sameness: it does not reflect the diversity and complexity of American life, not to mention the rest of the world.

Let us imagine that we are living at the end of the first dec-ade of this century. Victorian mores seem to be giving way to Edwardian explorations. We have just finished reading a scan-dalous novel by Theodore Dreiser, and we have had a sensible discussion about it with our parents at the dinner table. No-body has imagined World War I. And when we are in bed, thinking about the internal combustion engine, we hear, some-where in the night, a disturbance. We listen closely and it is a man saying the word *television* over and over. We go outside in our night clothes, and we track the figure down by the happy sound of his voice. He tells us that within forty years a square box with a glassy screen will arrive, at a price every-body can afford, and on this screen pictures will appear and inside the box voices will resonate. He is quite serious when he tells us that television will be every bit as significant as Gutenberg's printing press. He says that television will tell us stories every night, and that it will be a means of providing in-formation, of making the political process more visible, of con-necting us to new varieties of experience. We look forward to it.

What this excited optimist did not foresee is the situation

where on almost every night of the week, in the normal three-station city with its three network-affiliated broadcasters, there is nothing for people to watch but game shows or situation comedies or "action" crime shows that are patent copies of one another.

In 1938, a decade before the advent of commercial television in America, E. B. White saw his first demonstration of the invention. "I believe television is going to be the test of the modern world," he wrote, "and that in this new opportunity to see beyond the range of our vision we shall discover either a new and unbearable disturbance of the general peace or a saving radiance in the sky. We shall stand or fall by television—of that I am quite sure."

Television has clearly brought us closer to general disturbance than to celestial radiance, although it enabled us to watch men walk on the moon 240,000 miles away. Unfortunately, another 240,000 miles is taken up annually with identical automobile chases—a trail littered with smashed cars and ketchup-stained bodies, the endings made "meaningful" by identical solemn fadeouts.

The lack of diversity in entertainment programming has finally reached the point where the industry is parodying itself. In February of 1977, WNEW-TV, a New York nonnetwork station, placed a full-page ad in the *New York Times*. It pictured a middle-aged wife reading a program guide and asking her pot-bellied husband, who was looking at the television screen, "Tell me again, Larry, the bald detective with the dirty rain-coat and the white bird on his shoulder . . . which channel is he on?" Beneath the picture was the legend: "The networks are like one big station: WNBCBSABC. When one network invents a program, the others follow. Detectives chase detectives. Women with funny first names are appearing everywhere. Soon, there will be a bionic community. It goes on and on." After referring to "packaged laughter flowing on the networks," and "the networks playing cops and robbers," the ad makes its pitch: "Channel 5 [the independent station] offers you a choice." Of course, what WNEW-TV didn't tell you is that the choice is no choice; they show reruns. For reasons that we shall examine later on, the shows that receive the highest ratings are repeats of those same carbon-copy network shows, the only difference being that the independent station runs episodes of the same network series five days a week instead of once a week.

Decades ago the culinary experts who operated the Harvard freshman dining halls saw fit to have an artistically printed menu at every student's plate prior to service of the meal. We often wondered why they went to this trouble, since there were seldom any changes in the bill of fare. One evening we found that one of our fellow scholars had scribbled "Hebrews 13:8" on every menu. Immediately after lunch we repaired to the nearest available Bible to find the reference: "Jesus Christ the same yesterday, and today, and forever."

How the network monopoly works, how it makes for a mindless sameness in programs, how it perpetuates itself, and what if anything can be done about it—that's what this book is about. For make no mistake: whatever is bad and good about our daily televised fare is attributable to the network monopoly system. Some laymen like to blame "an advertiser-supported medium" for the ills of TV, implying that greedy sponsors dictate low-brow program content; others indict "moronic second-echelon vice-presidents" as the villains. The matter is not so simple. Advertisers have had little or nothing to say about program content for fifteen years, and when they did, they often used their influence to obtain better shows, regardless of lower audience ratings, because of the beneficial effect on their corporate or product image. And although it is true that some network programming vice-presidents are less than geniuses, their salaries and tenure depend on how well they carry out the demands of their superiors for ever-increasing profits. In short, TV programming is not the product of a gang of bad guys or good guys; it is determined by the relentless demands of a monopoly system.

Many television stations stay on the air twenty-four hours a day, and few broadcast less than eighteen. There are always people gazing at their sets, but the great bulk of the audience watches after the evening meal and prior to going to bed. The hours between 7:30 and 11:00 P.M. (6:30 and 10:00 in the Midwest), with some slight variations and with the strongest emphasis on the middle of that period, constitute the time when the "hut count" (that is not a census of substandard dwellings; "hut" stands for "homes using television") is at its peak. General principles governing television operation are applicable during all segments of a broadcast day, but because the economics of the industry have a dramatic relationship to the number of viewers, we shall concentrate on those periods (three and one-half hours per weeknight and an additional Sunday night half-hour) which are known as prime time.

THE NETWORKS

1

All for One and Three for All

"The public interest is what the public is interested in."
—Robert Sarnoff, while chief executive of NBC (1955–1965)

Webster defines monopoly as "exclusive ownership through legal privilege, command of supply, or concerted action."

The capitalist system works best where there is freedom to compete in an open market. Anyone can open a candy store, and since survival is subject to the fluctuations of supply and demand there is no need to artificially regulate the business. But not everyone can string up telephone and power lines or lay gas and water pipes in the ground—or send television images over the air. In these instances there is a practical barrier: there is no open market, there can be no "laissez-faire."

Monopolies are not necessarily all bad. In some areas the state actually fosters and protects them. Our patent and copyright laws allow the creator to keep his monopoly for a period of years. We encourage so-called "natural" monopolies such as the telephone and electric power; the government helps to create the monopoly and then goes about regulating its prices and

1

activities so that it cannot take unfair advantage of its economic omnipotence.

By the end of the nineteenth century it had become apparent that laws were needed to regulate big-business combinations (or trusts, as they were called) that could thwart competition and subvert the workings of a free-enterprise system. The first such law, the Sherman Anti-Trust Act, was passed in 1890. It is a brief statute, containing only a few sentences, but it became the foundation of succeeding acts of Congress and the large body of law that has since developed. In brief, it condemns "every person who shall monopolize, or attempt to monopolize . . . any part of the trade or commerce among the several states . . ."

Before he became the first commissioner of baseball, Kenesaw Mountain Landis was a federal district court judge whose chief claim to fame was that he had fined the Standard Oil Company one million dollars, the largest such criminal levy up to that time in the history of the United States. The company, under the direction of John D. Rockefeller, Sr., had been found guilty of attempting to monopolize the oil production and distribution business. It was the classic case of the greedy tycoon seeking to become the only buyer and the only seller of a vital commodity so that he could pay as little as possible and charge as much as possible, thus making as large a profit as possible. In recent years, practically every large company in America has been subjected to civil or criminal prosecution by the government, or to civil proceedings brought by their competitors under the antitrust laws.

Because, as we shall see, there cannot be more than three networks, our commercial television system is like a natural monopoly. Yet there is competition among the three, and it is this element of *competition within the monopoly* that, ironically, is mainly responsible for the sameness in programming.

If there were only one network, programming might be more diverse, and it certainly would be if there were a dozen networks. But the limitation to three seems to give us the worst of all possible worlds, because all three simultaneously direct their shows at an identical audience. A dreary similarity in subject matter and treatment is inevitable.

A profusion of networks would produce variety. In cities with numerous radio stations only a few of them specialize in rock and roll or "top forty" music. Others play classical music, country and western, or standards, and some are all "talk" or all news. The mass audience is so fractionalized that a broadcaster can do better with a large piece of a minority than with a small bit of the majority.

At the other extreme, if there were only one network, audience appeal could be more diverse because the pressure would be off. In some countries where television consists of a single network, usually government controlled, there is a much broader appeal to different tastes. This is not only because in many cases there is no commercial motivation, but because with what amounts to a captive audience there is no need to worry about being switched off for another station. But in America, with the aggressive competition among NBC, CBS, and ABC, all within the framework of the tight monopoly inherent in the network system, we wind up with both the evils of monopoly and the evils of competition, without the benefits of either.

What is the competition all about? To answer, we first have to understand something exciting about ourselves. Whenever we watch television we probably consider ourselves as part of a great audience, a wooed and desired prize. In one sense that is true. But in a larger and more realistic view, the reverse is true.

The advertiser on television wants us to buy his deodorant or detergent or automobile; that is, he hopes we will enter into a financial transaction with him in the future. But before we receive his message, a number of purchases have already occurred. The key one involved that same advertiser's paying thousands or hundreds of thousands of dollars in order to get the advertisement to us. Looking at that financial transaction, it becomes obvious that we, the television audience, are the commodity that is sold, the product that is bartered. We are examined, analyzed, and dissected—squeezed like the toilet paper, weighed like the steak, tested like the laundry soap.

In the creation of television programming, actors, writers, directors, cameramen, set designers, hairdressers, costumers, carpenters, electricians, stagehands, laboratory technicians, editors, lawyers, accountants, businessmen of all sorts, sell their services. The tape or film manufacturer sells his materials. The producer sells the finished show to the network. The network sells an ephemeral product called "time" to the advertiser.

American commercial television is advertiser supported. This means that in the final analysis the bill is paid by the sponsor. This is the financial transaction to end all financial transactions, the final and important step in this economic process. What the advertiser buys is the promise of an audience, its size, its demographic composition, its purchasing power. Within the advertising-agency fraternity the price of television exposure has been abbreviated as "C.P.M.," which means "cost per thousand." Per thousand what? Per thousand of us.

In his book *Television: The Business Behind the Box,* *New York Times* television critic Les Brown puts it succinctly: "The consumer, whom the custodians of the medium are pledged to serve, is in fact served up."

This troublesome truth has not always been so apparent as it is today. The economic patterns of television were anticipated by radio. During the quarter-century of radio dominance and the first decade of commercial video, advertisers, either directly or through their agencies, were literally "producers" of television entertainment, as well as of commercials. Sometimes they dealt through "independent producers" and sometimes they operated the production chores themselves. Traditionally they "controlled" various segments of time on one or more of the three national networks. They would take the program that they owned to the network, and pay the charges for the privilege of having it run, together with their commercial announcements, over the affiliated stations during the period set aside for their use.

In those days, intellectuals who disapproved of the mass-appeal content of radio and television programming tended to blame its shortcomings on the vulgar commercial motives of advertisers. There were numerous stories—for example, a General Motors or Chrysler sponsor refused to allow his agency to produce a program about Abraham Lincoln because his name advertised a rival automobile. Or a cigarette company vetoed a drama taking place in the Sahara Desert because of the inevitable mention of the beast of burden whose name was identified with a rival smoke.

As a matter of fact, when advertisers controlled programming there was greater diversity than there is today. Among certain advertisers there were exceptions to the quest for sheer numbers, and this served to keep on the air some programs that appealed to a small audience. One such series was the

"Firestone Hour," a program of classical and standard popular music that had been on radio for twenty years. It was taken over by television but eventually denied renewal of its time period by the network because it had steadily lost rating points to competing action-adventure shows. The sponsor publicly expressed its unhappiness, saying it would have supported the show indefinitely.

Other advertisers expressed similar resentment at the shift from sponsor to network control. Testifying before the FCC Network Study Committee in 1959, a man named Peter Levathes, who had been advertising-agency executive for the Kaiser Aluminum Company account, made the point that "in some instances, even though an advertiser is up against a 'strong' program on another network, he may well be satisfied with a smaller audience if he is reaching the type of audience to whom his product is salable. . . . In other words, while 'ratings' and size of audience are always factors which are considered, there may be situations where they may be outweighed by other factors such as cost, the type of audience or simply the judgment of the advertiser and his agency that his needs are being served by a particular program at a particular time."

Levathes went on to describe the "Kaiser Aluminum Hour," a program of sophisticated drama that ran on NBC opposite "The $64,000 Question," a high-rated CBS quiz show that later became a casualty of the "fix" scandal. Kaiser was willing to continue its program although, as Levathes testified,

> their audience was much smaller than that of "The $64,000 Question." However, NBC took the position that it could not afford to continue such a low-rated program in that time period because of its effect on the NBC audience for the balance of

the evening. This is the operation of a concept of "audience flow." In other words, it was NBC's position that the large shift of audience to CBS occasioned by "The $64,000 Question" adversely affected the total audience that NBC could deliver for the balance of the evening. Thus, NBC suggested and later demanded that Young & Rubicam [the advertising agency] and Kaiser agree to shift their program ... so that NBC could put into the vacated time period a program which NBC felt could match the highly successful "$64,000 Question" program. Both Kaiser and Young & Rubicam declined the demand of NBC, arguing that Kaiser had been willing to risk $4,000,000 for [its] program and felt that [it] was making headway in gaining increases in viewership or audience. Neither Kaiser nor Young & Rubicam were successful.

The reason why a network today will not program a series that it doesn't believe can garner a large audience, even if a sponsor will pay for it, is the "flow of audience" principle to which Levathes referred. The essence of the theory is that the American people are too lazy to get up and switch the dial once it is set. In their book *Television Economics,* Dr. Bruce M. Owen of Stanford, Dr. Jack H. Beebe of FRS Associates (an economics consulting firm), and Dr. Willard G. Manning, Jr., of Harvard, put it more politely: "The audience is believed to be passive, switching channels only as a result of rather extreme provocation." This leads to the commonly expressed belief of network executives that the audience for any program "depends to a very significant extent on the popularity of adjacent programs, as well as on the nature of the program itself."

Because we glibly describe television as a "mass" medium, we sometimes persuade ourselves that there really is a single homogeneous mass that consists of the vast majority of Americans. In matters of sensibility there probably is no such thing as a majority in this country. We are a nation of many differences—of size, age, weight, color, ethnic background, political persuasion, religion, economic means, education. The phrase "lowest common denominator" simply means the largest fraction that can include a certain group. It is undoubtedly true that more people like rock-and-roll music than opera, but it does not follow that a majority of all Americans like rock and roll. It is also true that a majority watch commercial television, but it does not follow that some of them would not prefer different kinds of programs some of the time.

At about the time that the networks had obtained full control from the emasculated advertisers, the research experts came up with something they called the science of demographics. They told us that the decision makers, the purchasers of the great bulk of the products and services advertised on television, are women from ages eighteen to forty-nine. Almost overnight, the universally sought audience segment became smaller and more sharply defined. Programs that appealed to older people, to children, to people with countrified tastes all but completely disappeared, despite the high overall ratings of those shows.

Even though it had one of the few large audiences on ABC in 1971, the Lawrence Welk show was canceled. The network programmers said the program "skewed old," meaning that its attraction was to viewers over forty-nine. Many advertisers associated with the show would have been glad to stay with it, but ABC, heeding the flow-of-audience concept, feared that the elderly watchers would taint the entire evening and give them the image of a network for the aged. By a lucky accident the FCC decreed the "Prime-Time Access Rule" (of which more later) the year the Welk show was canceled, so Don Fedderson, its producer, arranged to have the program picked up by 150 separate television stations (by a process called syndication, which will also be discussed later) over which it has been playing to larger and probably older audiences than ever before.

Shortly after ABC dropped Welk, in effect telling its elderly viewers to "drop dead," CBS purged its evening lineup of what the programmers called bucolic shows. Such series as "Hee-Haw," "Mayberry R.F.D.," and "Beverly Hillbillies" were beating the competition in their time slots, but CBS and the advertising fraternity came to the conclusion that high ratings accumulated in the rural areas did not compensate for loss of viewers in the biggest cities, especially in those where CBS owns stations. And so viewers with "bucolic" tastes joined the elderly as non-persons.

Les Brown in *Television: The Business Behind the Box* tells the story:

> CBS had an excess of corn, and the company's top executives were concerned about it. Moreover, as the CBS hit shows grew older so did their audiences, and advertising agencies were courting more vigorously than ever the young consumer in the 18–49 age range. Programs attractive to persons over fifty were becoming increasingly hard to sell to sponsors ... Bulk circulation, which once had been all-important to the networks, was becoming irrelevant.

With the exception of programs like sports events aimed at a male audience, the emphasis is on women from eighteen to forty-nine, with all other elements of our "mass" suffering some degree of disenfranchisement. The networks' willingness to sacrifice total audience size to obtain demographic purity appears even more significant in view of the high stakes. For the fierce competitive battle among the three giants is reflected not only on their respective balance sheets, but on the value of their stock on Wall Street.

If one of the three networks is dominant in prime time, it can earn, as clear net profit, from 50 to 100 million dollars more per year than either of its two competitors. In 1977, for example, first-place ABC reported a $63 million profit edge over third-place NBC, almost all of which is attributable to higher payments for prime-time commercial announcements. Comparative program costs usually don't vary between networks; it costs no more to develop a hit show than a failure. Figure it out for yourself: Suppose network A with a hit half-hour gets $90,000 per 30-second announcement, and network B with only a moderately successful show gets $50,000 per 30-second announcement. (These figures are taken from the 1977–78 history of ABC's high-rated "Three's Company" as compared with NBC's so-so "C.P.O. Sharkey," programs with practically identical production costs.) Now with three minutes to sell, network A is ahead $240,000 each week (leavened by a $36,000 higher advertising-agency commission) or more than $10 million on the year for just one half-hour, which is one forty-second of prime time!

In the mid 1960s, when the dollar was worth more than twice what it is today, a financial analyst named David Blank estimated that a single rating point during prime time was worth $10 million. Is it any wonder that the top officers of the networks aspire to higher ratings, better demographics, and bigger numbers? Neither balance nor diversity matters; the demand is simply for shows that will strengthen the ratings. Network executives have made a public virtue of this drive. They use it to answer criticism of mediocrity, shoddiness, and sameness in their programming. Frank Stanton was president of CBS from its beginning until his retirement in 1973. Because of the frequency and polished brilliance of his testimony before congressional committees he acquired a reputation as statesman of the broadcasting industry. Here are some excerpts from his testimony before a Senate investigating committee.

In reply to the charge that three network presidents "exercise an arbitrary and capricious power" over what the public sees, he said, "They do no such thing." Like any other corporation, Stanton said his had "final responsibility of deciding, and the decision is based on the company's best information of the needs and wants of the consuming public."

Lest there be any doubt as to what "consuming public" meant, Stanton explained CBS's duty to the public:

> ... to satisfy the tastes of the public and to expose it to the widest variety of information, entertainment, and art so that, if it chooses, the public may develop new and different tastes. ...
> In fact, in the business of broadcasting, perhaps more than in any other business, the ultimate decision is not ours but the public's. In our business the process is one of pure democracy. ... It is absolutely impossible for networks or their officers to affront public taste, to deny public taste, to control public taste, to run persistently counter to public taste, or to manipulate public taste to their own ends. For television, the public is

the ultimate monitor—the monitor-in-chief. What it persistently turns off, cannot be turned on again by any group of network executives.

What "public" was Stanton referring to? Was he including children or the old in that highly elastic term? Or was he simply referring to those people who watch anything as long as it's on the tube? Which of the public's "tastes" did he mean? How did Stanton know what the "public" wanted before he delivered it to them?

Robert Sarnoff was president of NBC while Stanton was at CBS. Like Stanton, Sarnoff was unable to define his terms clearly. Before the same congressional committee he said, "We must understand that it is a minority distaste for programs chosen by a majority that has triggered the slogan of mediocrity—and we must label this slogan for what it really is, a failure to respect freedom of taste, an effort of the few to impose their tastes on the many."

Who imposes whose tastes on whom? How can television executives claim to know what the people want when the people themselves can't know what they want? As Michael Arlen has said in *The View from Highway 1*, "If a reader cannot, in advance, conceive of *Moby Dick* on his own, how should he ask the culture to somehow provide such a work?"

A few years ago an executive of one of the networks turned down a dramatic series set in an African locale, after viewing the pilot film. "Hell, it's a nigger series," he said. "The American people won't watch a show about blacks." Then, early in 1977, ABC took a chance on a "mini-series," just eight episodes, based on Alex Haley's book *Roots*. The story began in a farming village in Gambia, West Africa, with incidents from the lives of Haley's ancestors, and then moved to America, where it vividly depicted the horrors and injustices suffered by blacks under slavery. The programs got the highest rating in the history of television. Nielsen estimated that the last episode went into over 36 million homes and was seen by 80 million people with a total of 130 million watching all or part of the series. The network executive was neither the first nor the last programmer to confuse omnipotence with omniscience.

Russell Baker, the "Observer" of the *New York Times,* was struck by the paradox of network leaders arguing that "their nocturnal production of mayhem is a simple case of giving people what they want." If people knew what they wanted, he reasoned, "there would never be a television commercial made." The purpose of commercials, he said, "is to make people want things they hadn't thought of wanting until the commercial went to work on their desire juices. . . . A good salesman makes the customer want what he has to sell. . . . There is a strong smell of insincerity in their insistence that the customer must call the shots when the entertainment starts. . . . Since most people do not have the faintest notion what they want, it is ridiculous to argue that you are merely giving it to them. Almost everybody knows very clearly what he does not want, on television as in life. Knowing what you do not want does not, however, mean that you know what you do want."

In 1973, research experts discovered that (shades of McLuhan) people really are more interested in the medium than in the message. People don't watch shows; they watch *television.* They watch the tube every night, regardless of what's on. And that means that they don't necessarily watch what they like; they look at what they *dislike least* among the programs proffered at the time.

Gerbner and Gross report it this way:

> The total viewing audience is fairly stable regardless of what is on. Individual tastes and program preferences are less important in determining viewing patterns than is the time a program is on. The nearly universal, non-selective, and habitual use of television fits the ritualistic pattern of its programming. You watch television as you might attend a church service, except that most people watch television more religiously.

A ratings review undertaken by the President's Office of Telecommunications Policy in 1973 produced astonishing results. The researchers examined national ratings for the month of April in each of the twenty consecutive years from 1953 to 1972. They found that the percentage of homes where sets were in use during prime time remained almost constant, regardless of week or year or whatever was on the air at the time. The average tune-in was about 60 percent of all television homes, going to a high of 62 percent in 1957 and a low of 57.3 percent in 1963. This persisted despite the many changes in patterns and types of entertainment that occurred during that twenty-year span. For example, during the first of those two decades, only first-run shows were telecast by the networks in April. With a pattern of from thirty-six to thirty-nine new episodes to cover fifty-two weeks, the repeat cycle didn't start much before June. But during the later years, practically all series episodes on network television during April were repeats of shows shown earlier in the year, the number of new segments to cover a year's order having shrunk from twenty-six to twenty-four and most recently to twenty-two. But viewers watched TV in the same numbers, whether they were watching new shows or reruns.

Paul Klein used to be vice-president of NBC for audience measurement; more recently, he was vice-president for programming. Between those two jobs he wrote occasional magazine articles. In one such article in *New York* (January 25, 1971) he discussed this phenomenon, calling it the Theory of the Least Objectionable Program, or "L.O.P." After pointing out that people in 36 million homes are watching TV in prime time at any given moment, with the three networks commanding over 91 percent of this audience (independent and educational stations draw less than 9 percent), he commented on what he called its "amazingly constant size" regardless of whether the network shows at a given hour "are strong, weak, so-so, or one of each."

To Klein this means that we, the viewers, watch television "because it's there." We watch one show rather than another because it

can be endured with the least amount of pain and suffering. You view television irrespective of the content of the program watched. And because the programs are designed to appeal to the greatest number of people—rich and poor, smart and stupid, tall and short, wild and tame—you're probably watching something that is not *your* taste. Nevertheless, you take what is fed to you because you are compelled to exercise the medium. ... The best network programmers understand this. They are not stupid. They like most of the stuff they put on about as much as you do. But they also know that a program doesn't have to be "good." It only has to be less objectionable than whatever the hell the other guys throw against it.

Klein finds further applications of his L.O.P. theory. It explains, he says, why some new and likable performers don't last, while some older and more tired hands hang on indefinitely. And, he adds, "L.O.P. explains why some interesting programs die and some stupid programs seem to thrive. Place a weak show against weaker competition, L.O.P. teaches us, and it inevitably looks good; it may even look like a hit—get huge ratings and a quality audience if the time period it fills has that audience. Place a strong show against a stronger show, and, never mind whether it is far superior to a dozen other shows on the air in other time slots, it will look like a bomb."

Finally, there is the inevitable comparison between L.O.P. and a presidential campaign. In politics we are used to voting for the "lesser of two evils" and we accept that as a necessary adjunct of the two-party system. We recognize that our country is so heterogeneous, the people's interests so varied, and the political issues so many and so complex, that if any one candidate took a solid stand on most of the important current questions, he would have to antagonize all but a small group of faithful believers. The result is that candidates of both parties tend toward the middle and appear quite similar in their views.

Under a multiparty system the candidates can be sharp and outspoken on a multitude of matters, but then, as is the case in a number of European countries, government functions only through coalition. The government sometimes winds up with a complexion not unlike our own. Under the two-party system we do our coalescing before the campaign rather than after the election.

The political arena is similar to the television game in that the two major parties, like the three networks, strive to attract the largest audience they can, to satisfy the greatest number, to antagonize as few people as possible. But there is one important difference. The political parties each try to represent a different fundamental philosophy. But the three networks all have the same philosophy: to get the biggest buck.

2

The Making of
the Monopoly

*"We have rejected government ownership of broadcasting stations, believing
that the power inherent in control over broadcasting is too great and too dangerous to the maintenance of free institutions to permit its exercise by one
body, even though elected by or responsible to the whole people. But in
avoiding the concentration of power over radio broadcasting in the hands of
government, we must not fall into an even more dangerous pitfall: the concentration of that power in the hands of self-perpetuating management
groups."*

—The Federal Communications Commission in 1941

Two fundamental facts must be understood about the operation of American commercial television: it is a business operated for profit, and there is a limit on the number of available
broadcast channels.

There is no need to elaborate on the first point. One should
simply keep in mind at all times that television executives are
accountable to their investors and stockholders, not to their
critics.

It is the second point that is not always appreciated. The unpleasant truth is that there cannot be more than three networks, because there is no place to put them. That is a result of

scientific circumstance, but, paradoxically, it need not have been that way.

A television program is transmitted over air waves. Fifty years ago, with the development of commercial radio, it was recognized that private concerns operating at will through the ether created confusion. By 1927 uncontrolled radio transmissions had created such a pandemonium of broadcast blasts and squeals that Congress was forced to act with uncharacteristic haste to halt the anarchy. It created the Federal Radio Commission with full and exclusive authority to license all radio transmitters and require them to adhere to their assigned use of power and hours of operation, and to stay within their channels, or "frequencies." Seven years later that statute was amended and replaced by the Communications Act of 1934, and the name of the administering agency was changed to the Federal Communications Commission. That bureau and that law govern television today.

In the case of radio, the basic problem was one of channeling traffic rather than creating highways. Although certain vested interests succeeded for a few years in restricting the number of radio-transmitting stations, the problem was truly one of allocation, that is, of assigning an available frequency to each applicant in a manner that would prevent physical overlap or involuntary jamming.

Unfortunately, television developed quite differently. Very High Frequency (VHF) transmission, which comprised only what we know as the first thirteen channels, was the sole system perfected and ready when the Federal Communications Commission authorized the first commercial television service in 1941. There was no general use of television for another six years because of the intervention of World War II.

It was during the war that the uses of the UHF (Ultra High Frequency) band became known. A little more than a month after the Japanese surrendered, on August 15, 1945, the FCC considered the possibility of substituting UHF for VHF. It was recognized that the thirteen channels thought to be available in the VHF frequency were insufficient to provide a nationwide service comparable to that available for radio. The proponents of UHF urged delay until they could demonstrate the practical applicability of sets made to receive signals in that band.

Strangely enough, the leading argument for a delay to prove the efficacy of UHF came from the Columbia Broadcasting System. CBS was busily experimenting with color television, using a design that would operate only in the UHF band, and, anxious to establish its technical superiority, it pleaded for the time to prove that its system would work. RCA led the opposition, saying that the time was ripe for the development of commercial television and that deferment would be unwise, especially since the extent of any delay was unknown.

VHF television at that time was entirely black and white; a decade was to pass before color TV would be perfected and sold to the public. But in 1946, UHF was pushed on the grounds that it could provide immediate color television. The FCC considered the problem for over a year. Should we, they asked, have black and white television immediately, or shall we wait the indeterminate amount of time necessary to start out with color television? The broader implications of the larger number of channels available in UHF were a secondary consideration, seldom mentioned.

In March of 1947 the FCC finally made its decision, denying the CBS request for delay and opting for the immediate use of what they described as thirteen VHF channels. It turned out to be a fateful decision, not because of the question of color or delay, but because it limited, perhaps forever, the number of channels, thus creating a television monopoly in the United States. Overnight, millions of television sets capable of receiving only VHF were made and sold, and the companies that were later to control this industry were granted allocations within the thirteen-channel band. This created the vested interests and power combinations that were almost immediately to prove so strong and so important that they eluded any real attempts at control on the part of the public, either directly or through governmental agencies. Little did CBS know at the time how much it gained by losing the UHF argument.

Throughout the discussions and proceedings, all of the interested parties and the members of the FCC had described VHF as consisting of thirteen channels. The final FCC decision to ignore UHF was close, and it is conceivable that it might have gone the other way had the commissioners realized that there would not even be as many as thirteen channels. Within five months, however, it became obvious that channel 1 was unusable. The interference that it caused with various other frequencies made it necessary for the FCC to retire channel 1 to uses not connected with commercial television.

And thereby hangs another bit of irony. For one of the cities to which channel 1 had been allocated was Trenton, New Jersey. The retirement of channel 1 meant that it would be impossible for the state of New Jersey, the eighth largest in the country, to have a VHF television station within its borders, a dereliction which plagues that commonwealth, as well as the members of the FCC, to this day.

The UHF agitation did not die down. In early 1948 the FCC was urged to reopen the allocations for what was now described as "black-and-white UHF." But the fear that such a move would make obsolete all those millions of television sets that had just been manufactured and paid for by trusting citizens was too powerful a deterrent. The FCC stumbled out of the difficulty in October 1948 by announcing a "freeze" on all further allocations. This freeze, which originally was announced to last ninety days, lasted for three and one-half years; it was not until April 1952 that allocations were reopened and the first assignments made in the UHF band. By that time it was, as we shall see, too late. The virtually irrevocable pattern had been established. It was as though the conditions that assure a three-network monopoly had been hardened into concrete that would be impervious to the scratches of the few ineffectual latecomers.

Coincident with its early channel assignments, the FCC announced its policy of localism. Borrowed from radio, this concept limited the creation of powerful regional transmitters designed to cover a broad area in favor of small but more numerous stations allocated on a city-by-city basis. The stated purpose was to maximize the opportunity for local self-expression by communities. Though well suited to radio with its plethora of available frequencies, this policy turned out to be less than ideal for television. Not only was the spectrum limited to twelve channels, but the commission soon learned that to prevent interference each television station using the same numbered channel had to be separated by approximately two hundred miles.

The result is that the great majority of United States cities are served by no more than three VHF stations. There is no way to get any more. New York and Los Angeles are unusual in that each has seven VHF stations. No other city has more than four and there are only thirteen cities, some of which are not extremely large, that have four stations. The populous market areas whose centers are Philadelphia, Boston, Detroit, Cleveland, Cincinnati, Houston, Pittsburgh, Baltimore, Milwaukee, Kansas City, and Buffalo each have three commercial VHF stations, and some others have only two. Hence, it is evident that there cannot be more than three networks (and in some cities a station will actually have to take programs from more than one network) as long as national television is geared to the VHF band.

For economic reasons, as we shall see, almost all network outlets are VHF stations. Because seventy additional channels would have altered the structure of television considerably, it is important to ask why it never happened.

On July 1, 1952, the FCC lifted its freeze and began issuing construction permits for UHF stations. Because of the availability of seventy new channels, the commission put 1,319 UHF licenses on the counter, as opposed to the 556 with which it had exhausted the VHF supply. Many of the new permits which hopeful entrepreneurs applied for were never picked up. Of the 153 UHF stations that actually went on the air over the next four years, 63 went bankrupt, and all but a handful of the remainder shut down in failure—this in an industry of almost guaranteed prosperity, where bankruptcy of a VHF station is literally unheard of.

Why the debacle? In the first place, the UHF stations couldn't get an audience, because most viewers were not equipped to receive their signal. When the FCC announced its allocations freeze in 1948, there were one million receiving sets in the country. When the hiatus ended in 1952, there were seventeen million sets, none of which could tune in to a UHF signal. Four years later that number had increased to thirty-seven million sets, but only 18 percent of them—fewer than seven million—had UHF-receiving capability.

Then, as now, the manufacturing and marketing of television sets was a highly competitive business. A manufacturer could not compete if he added an unnecessary gadget to his more popular models, and the device required for UHF reception was regarded as such a gadget.

The set owner could buy a "converter" for this purpose, but why should he spend the money? What would he get in return? The independent UHF stations weren't able to offer programming that he wanted to see. The UHF station operator was caught in a "chicken or egg" dilemma. Without programming, he couldn't attract an audience; without an audience, he couldn't appeal to an advertiser; without an advertiser, he couldn't get the money to buy programming—even assuming it was available.

In a city where a UHF station tried to compete with a VHF station, a sort of reverse Gresham's law went into effect. A typical example was a city with two or three VHF stations and no more frequencies available on the VHF band. Applicants for additional channels were granted UHF licenses, and when the first one went on the air the market consisted of two or three VHFs and one UHF station. VHF having arrived there first, the viewers had sets that could not bring in the UHF signals. Even where the UHF station was the first to go on the air, and all the local receivers were able to tune in the signal, the later arrival of VHF stations often proved fatal. The VHF stations brought in network programs, and as set sales increased, the UHF station gradually declined. During the four-year period following the lifting of the freeze, sixteen of the thirty-one

UHF stations that had been pioneers in cities later invaded by VHF stations were forced off the air.

The FCC and Congress tried to help the UHF spectrum become viable. The FCC had enforced the rule that no single entity could own more than five television stations. In 1954 it announced a relaxation of that rule extending the limit to seven stations, provided that at least two of them were UHFs. The most important station-group owners were the networks, and almost immediately CBS and NBC tried the experiment of adding two UHF stations to the five VHF stations they already owned. Both networks bought UHF stations in Hartford, Connecticut, which appeared to be a promising area because there was only one VHF station in that city and the nearest VHF competition came from an ABC affiliate in New Haven, forty miles away. CBS also bought the only UHF in Milwaukee, and NBC bought the only UHF in Buffalo. Both networks poured their economic strength and prestige into these operations, but after four years they gave up the ghost. All four stations were sold.

CBS's president Frank Stanton admitted failure: "We put everything we could think of behind management, in terms of facilities, money, promotion, everything else, because I was dedicated to trying to show the world that we could make it work." About the Milwaukee experiment he was more blunt: "UHF simply can't compete with two or more VHF's."

In 1963, Congress tried to help by passing the "all-channel set" law, which decreed that after May 1, 1964, no new TV set could be shipped in interstate commerce (meaning, in effect, that no new set could be manufactured) unless it could receive UHF signals. This helped somewhat; as a result of the all-channel law, UHF was rescued from oblivion and raised to its present status of second-class citizen.

Aside from the problem of competitive programming, there are still practical difficulties for the television viewer who wants to watch UHF stations. He must install a separate antenna to pick up the UHF signals, and it must be oriented in the direction of UHF transmitters. (This is why the transmitting towers are usually clustered together in a single area of an urban community, commonly known as an "antenna farm.") Also, the UHF signal does not carry as far or with the same intensity as a VHF signal. Finally, to receive the UHF signal one must carefully turn the dial, or "fine tune"; with VHF one simply punches in (so-called detent tuning). Congress belatedly took steps in 1976 to correct this error by amending the all-channel law so that the detent tuning device now adorns all new receivers. Given all these difficulties, it is not surprising that UHF remains a poor relation in any city where it must compete with VHF. There are approximately seven hundred commercial television outlets in the United States, about one hundred of which are in the UHF band—this, in spite of the fact that there are seventy channels available in UHF and only twelve in VHF.

In each of the cities that it covers, a network operates through a television station that is either "affiliated" with it (by means of contract) or "owned and operated" by it. Approximately 85 percent of commercial television stations are affiliated with NBC, CBS, or ABC. This means that on the average, over a full broadcast day, 60 percent of their programming is supplied directly by the network; during the last three hours of prime time the figure is almost 100 percent.

Obviously, with three networks, a city that has three or fewer television stations will not have any outlet that is not either affiliated with or owned and operated by a network. Unaffiliated stations are called independent stations, and there are only fifteen cities in the United States that have any commercial independent VHF stations.

Because of the inability of UHF stations to command an audience commensurate with that offered by VHF, the three networks uniformly refuse to license a UHF station as an affiliate in any city in which there are three or more VHF outlets. The few cities where UHF stations are network affiliates have either no VHF stations or only one or two. For twenty years ABC was affiliated with a VHF station located in Mexico in preference to a UHF station in the United States. San Diego's two VHFs were affiliated with CBS and NBC. ABC preferred to affiliate with XEWT, a VHF in Tijuana, rather than the UHF in San Diego, until a nationalistic FCC recommended the change.

The problems of UHF accrete like the proverbial rolling snowball. Because it has fewer viewers, the networks avoid it whenever possible in making affiliation contracts. UHF programming, therefore, tends to specialize in old movies, off-network reruns, and secondary products that draw few viewers. Since advertisers buy on a cost-per-thousand-viewers basis, they pay a UHF station less than they pay a VHF one for the same announcement. This contributes to the inability of UHF to improve its programming.

In summary, we can state that UHF stations have been able to prosper in three situations:

1. In all-UHF markets (Fresno and Bakersfield, California; South Bend and Fort Wayne, Indiana; Scranton–Wilkes Barre, Pennsylvania; Peoria, Illinois; Lexington, Kentucky; Youngstown, Ohio; Yakima, Washington; Elmira, New

York; and Huntsville, Alabama are the only cities where there is no VHF competition).

2. Where they are network affiliates (usually because there are not sufficient VHF stations to take care of the three networks, as in San Diego, Louisville, Toledo, Hartford, and Madison, Wisconsin).

3. As independent stations in the twenty-five largest cities, especially where there is no nonnetwork VHF (Cleveland, Cincinnati, Atlanta, Detroit).

Over the past two decades there have been numerous attempts to start a fourth network, which would transmit over independent stations throughout the country. These plans always called for utilization of independent VHF stations in New York, Los Angeles, Chicago, San Francisco, Washington, Seattle, Portland, Minneapolis, St. Louis, Indianapolis, Denver, Dallas, Miami, Tucson, and Phoenix. But in all other cities, including Philadelphia, Boston, Detroit, Cleveland, Pittsburgh, Baltimore, Cincinnati, Hartford-Springfield, Tampa, Houston, Atlanta, Kansas City, Buffalo, Columbus, Milwaukee, and perhaps one hundred others, the "fourth network" is faced with the necessity of either going to UHF or not having an outlet in the market. Because of the low drawing power of independent UHF stations, these attempts have failed. There was simply no way to make the total number of viewers add up to the sufficient thousands necessary to attract the advertising revenue that pays for programming and other costs.

In 1977 there was a revival of conversation among the less experienced members of the industry about a fourth network. It stemmed from the frustration of advertisers chafing under network exaction of increased payment for commercial time, a result of the networks' unprecedented prosperity in 1976.

Upon analysis the announced proposals turned out to be something less than the "limited network" they described.

One such proposal is indeed feasible, but the word *limited* is an understatement. It calls for the production of miniseries consisting of six one-hour shows, such as the dramatization of a popular novel. Network-affiliated stations across the land would be expected to preempt their regular fare for one hour on one night to carry the series. This proposal usurps less than 1 percent of a network's time, and there cannot be even so limited a slice unless affiliated stations are able and willing to knock off the programs of NBC, CBS, or ABC.

Another proposal calls for a "barter network." Under this plan, an advertiser pays the cost of production of a series of programs. He then takes the programs to television stations and gives them to the station free of charge, provided the station agrees to run announcements that use a portion of the allotted commercial time. The remainder of the commercial time is left to the station to sell. The planners of the 1977 series wanted to cover five nights each week; it was not expected that network affiliates would preempt for it, so it was aimed at independent stations. Because of the UHF situation, a complete sale would expose the series to, at best, half the American television homes. It was obviously impossible for such a series to compete for the audience with the network shows that would be on the air at the same time, and since the advertiser pays on the basis of viewers he expects to reach, and with this barter show he would only get half as many viewers, he could only pay about half as much. Producers will tell you that money may not be everything, but in the long run it does affect what shows up on the screen. The plan had to fail—and it did.

In a recent decision, Judge J. Edward Lumbard of the

United States Court of Appeals for the Second Circuit spoke of the "entry-proof market of television in which the three networks have a virtual monopoly on the type and quality of programs and ideas that are disseminated to the public." Twenty years before, CBS president Frank Stanton, testifying on September 24, 1956, before the Antitrust Subcommittee of the House Committee on the Judiciary, spoke of television's youth, saying, "We will reach full maturity on the day when we can find more room for more comparable station facilities."

Is television really an entryproof market? Or just doomed to permanent immaturity?

3

Ratings:
The "Lifeblood"

"The only places in the Republic where points and point spreads are given greater urgency than here in the casinos of Las Vegas are the corporate headquarters of the three networks in New York."
    —Charles D. Ferris, chairman of the Federal Communications Commission, before the National Association of Broadcasters convention, April 12, 1978

Program ratings are obtained through the A. C. Nielsen Company's service or the American Rating Bureau service (known as Arbitron). Nielsen selects what it considers a representative number of homes and attaches a machine called an audimeter to the television set in each of those homes. This machine automatically records the station to which the viewer tunes and the hour of the day when this tuning occurs. Arbitron operates with "diaries," which it distributes to representatively selected groups. In each case there is a periodic collection of the data.

The most quoted rating is the national Nielsen. Nielsen selects approximately 1,200 homes in the entire United States as the basis for its sampling. Yet the number of reports never measures up to the full 1,200; there are always some sets not reporting due to malfunction or because the owner is on vacation or for some other reason; 900 is probably closer to the accurate number. Nine hundred homes out of the 60 million that contain television sets would appear to the layman so small a sample as to be truly arbitrary. In reply the rating experts point out that the process is expensive, and the very slight advantage in degree of accuracy to be gained from adding to the sample does not justify the heavy costs it would involve. They insist that the increase in accuracy as the sample size increases is minuscule, that if you tested not 1,200 homes but 12,000 or even 120,000 this figure would still be considered small in relation to a 60-million base, and the degree of accuracy would not be materially changed.

A few years ago I was the Democratic candidate for Congress from the twenty-fifth district of New York. While my campaign was in the planning stages, I decided to poll some of my hoped-for constituents to ascertain what issues they considered important, what their views were on some controversial questions, and how well known my opponent (the incumbent) really was. An eager young research expert was my volunteer adviser on this project. There were about 200,000 votes in the district and I planned to send out 10,000 questionnaires.

My adviser was horrified.

"What's the trouble?" I asked. "Isn't the sampling big enough?"

"Big enough?" he exclaimed. "It's much too big. You will be the laughingstock of all research people."

James Lyons, president of the Media Research Services Group of A. C. Nielsen, did not make the mistake of claiming that a sample can be too large when he described the ratings process on an ABC broadcast on November 20, 1977. He compared the TV universe to a large bag of red, white, and black jellybeans, from which Nielsen repeatedly extracts a handful. "If I do that fifteen or twenty times," he said, "recording the black and red and white count each time, I'll get a pretty good estimate of the number in the entire bag." The analogy makes sense if we understand that the jellybeans do not represent people or even programs, but the viewers' choice among the three networks. The trouble is that too many network executives have shown by their public pronouncements that they believe the sampling shows that people prefer jellybeans that are red, white, or black to those of any other conceivable color; that people like jellybeans in general; and that they prefer jellybeans to any other type of nourishment.

Having considered the monetary value of each rating point to a network, let us consider what ratings mean to a producer. His major concern is the networks' use of the Nielsen ratings as the basis of comparison for programs shown in the same time period, the "share" of the actual viewing audience being of greater significance for him than the percentage of all potential viewers. From the producer's point of view, the smallness of the sample is more frustrating than even the ratio of nine hundred to all the television homes in America would make it appear. For example, let us use the trade's rule of thumb that a network series that gains a national share of 30 percent or more of the viewing audience is successful enough to warrant renewal for another year. Should the show not attract as many as 30 percent of the TV watchers during it time period, its logical fate is cancellation.

Now we aren't dealing with shows that get "0" or "100"—there never have been any such cases. We are dealing with three networks, each of which has a program that is seen by anywhere from 23 to 37 percent of the people who have their sets turned on. Let's assume, therefore, the common case of a series that is getting a 27 percent share according to the audimeters that are working in any one week (and for purposes of this example we'll assume that all 1,200 are reporting and that all viewers are watching network shows). If this program could be raised by only 5 points, from 27 percent to 32 percent, the difference would be equivalent to that of "triumphant success" as opposed to "dismal failure." Now with all 1,200 audimeters reporting, a shift of a mere 60 would constitute this great change. Think of it for a moment: sixty television homes out of sixty million television homes, or one family in every million families!

Now let's shift the scene and look at the stakes involved in getting this one family in a million to change the station. The average television series is made at a loss by the producer. The network pays him a certain sum for the network run (which includes some repeats), but when he adds it all together the producer finds that in order to satisfy the network's demand for ever-improving quality, he has to spend more money than he gets. This may seem like a fool's business—selling a product that costs you more than you are paid for it—but the producer is willing to gamble because of the possibility of a fairly large killing should the dice fall in the right way.

Sometimes the producer can minimize or even wipe out his losses by means of foreign sales. But so far as I know there have been no cases where any producer has gotten rich by making a prime-time series that ran only on the U.S. networks and in foreign countries and had no later set of repeats in the

United States. The big profit comes from postnetwork reruns in America.

In order to be successful in reruns, there must be a sufficient quantity of shows to "strip," a word that means broadcasting a different episode each day of the week, or at least during the five weekdays. The ideal is for a station to have enough episodes of a series so that a different one can be telecast each weekday for twenty weeks, without the necessity of running a repeat. This obviously requires 100 episodes. In the early days of television, 32 to 39 episodes were made each year, and by the end of 3 years there would be anywhere from 96 to 117 available in any single series. Today, however, with the networks reducing their yearly load to 22 episodes, it requires 5 years to get over 100 programs. If, for example, you have only three years of programming of a single series under modern conditions, this would give you 66 segments, and rerunning them at the rate of one every day of the week except Saturday and Sunday would mean that you would have used all but one of them in 13 weeks. Stations don't relish going into repeats 13 weeks after their first run—the public's memory is a little too sharp for that—hence the requirement of quantity as well as quality in the rerun series.

Stripping the reruns of successful series after they have completed their network exposure has become a staple of independent stations during prime time, and of network-affiliated stations in the afternoon and "fringe" time periods (that is, the hours on the fringes of prime time, both before and after).

The television industry's usage of the word *strip* comes to us from radio. I remember one day shortly after World War II describing such a program to the board of directors of the American Federation of Radio Artists, the union of performers for which I served as executive secretary. One of the more charming and intelligent members of the board was the reformed burlesque queen Gypsy Rose Lee. When I mentioned the term *strip* show, Gypsy's eyes widened and she exclaimed, "Oh my God! Not in radio too."

It is conceivable that some series are so good that even without a strippable quantity of episodes they might be sold on a one-per-week basis for rebroadcast in the United States, but this seldom if ever happens, because the residual costs (the payments that the producer has to make to the unions representing the actors, writers, directors, and musicians, plus the additional payments he must make under contracts that he entered into with his star performers) are such that they simply cannot be made up by one-per-week sales in the few cities where such deals might be made. Because the networks today order only twenty-two episodes of a series per year, there must be at least four and preferably five or more years of a series run on network in prime time before the producer hits this long-awaited jackpot.

Let's take a typical example: a half-hour situation comedy on tape, for which the network pays the producer an average of $150,000 per show (the first year he gets $143,000, the second year $150,000, the third year $157,000, etc.). The costs of the show are such that even with the escalating price, the producer loses about $15,000 per show; the actual cost to him averages $165,000 each. Foreign sales will cut his loss only slightly, because American situation comedies are not big sellers abroad—most foreign viewers do not appreciate the American sense of humor—and since the series is made on tape, there are technical difficulties that make foreign sales less likely.

There are two types of technical difficulties. First, most countries outside the United States and Canada operate with a different recording and broadcasting technique from ours.

They use 625-line tape instead of 525-line tape, which requires an expensive transfer process for adjustment, a cost not easily justified. Second, with a tape show, all sound is recorded simultaneously with the photography of the action; in film, the music and sound effects are dubbed in after the action and dialogue are shot. Thus, in the case of film there is a separate music-and-effects sound track that can be used with a foreign-language dialogue track. It is impossible, however, to put a foreign language into a tape show without destroying the music and sound effects and requiring an entirely new, costly scoring and sound-effects session.

In view of such show costs and foreign-sales problems it is safe to say that the producer will not net more than about $5,000 per episode from foreign sales after he has paid all of the costs and distribution fees, thus cutting his loss to $10,000 per episode. If he has been on the air for three years he will have made sixty-six episodes, and will be in the hole to the tune of $660,000.

That's where he will wind up if he doesn't get a fourth year on the network in prime time. On the other hand, if the show should go four years, the chances are that it will be renewed for a fifth, and in either event he will have enough episodes for rerun stripping. Now let's assume that the show stays on a network for five years, that he first gets a stripping deal for a morning slot on the network at a price that is sufficient to pay all of his union and other residual costs to cover a future of six to ten reruns. Upon the conclusion of the network's stripping deal he now sells the show to individual stations for further stripping on a local basis. Judging by current prices, he will gross at least $100,000 per episode from United States reruns. Allowing for as much as half of this amount to go as a fee to his distributor and for various costs of tapes and advertising and shipping, with 5 years of product, or 110 episodes, he will clear $5.5 million for himself. Subtracting the $440,000 production loss on the additional two years of shows, he still has over $5 million in net profit.

Let's return now to the moment when the show ends its third year and the network must make the decision about renewing. The difference to the producer will be a $660,000 loss on the one hand or a $5 million gain on the other. We know that if the series has been getting 27 percent of the available audience it will not be renewed, whereas if it has been getting a share of 32 percent it will be renewed. And that decision—that $5 million—depends on the switch of a dial by sixty people.

Put yourself in the position of that producer: what wouldn't you give to be able to find those few people who can make this tremendous change in your life? To be able to turn a $660,000 loss into a $5 million profit—what would it mean to you? Would it be worth a million dollars? Two million dollars? Maybe more? If you could only find out who has the audimeters, you wouldn't need to bribe them. A few dollars might buy the kind of influence that could be brought to bear on these viewers to switch to your show. People with whom they come in contact, a friend or relative or maybe a tradesman, says, "You'd better watch X show tonight. I hear it's great." Or maybe the milkman or someone hired to come to the door in the guise of a house-to-house salesperson drops the important suggestion to the important people at the important time.

The temptation to corruption in any industry is commensurate with the financial stakes involved. There have been rumors of payoffs and bribes to various network officials, including network presidents who could make programming decisions. And in the days when producers sold series directly to advertisers through their agencies, there were many stories of expensive "gifts" as well as outright financial bribery to agency account executives who could make the key recommendations. Sometimes the producer would write off the costs of these illegal benefits as a business expense by purchasing the outline of a series idea from the recipient. Nobody in the Internal Revenue Service would be able to judge the value of a series idea, and no revenue agent could insist that he knew more about such values than an experienced producer who was constantly buying ideas and presentations that would never go beyond their initial paper stage. Thus, by writing off the cost of the gifts as a business expense, the corruptor could get Uncle Sam to pay half the value of the handsome pourboire that had been given to the corruptee.

The rating services insist that their security measures are so tight that there can be no violation of the confidentiality of their lists. However, in March 1963 a subcommittee of the Special Investigations Committee of the House of Representatives commenced a series of hearings on the subject of television rating services. The announced reason for the hearings was to ascertain the truth or falsity of rumors of "fraud, misrepresentation, and coercion" in the services. There was much testimony, but nothing substantial developed. After a Nielsen representative had attempted to describe his use of a weighting factor in national reports to adjust the sets-in-use levels in local reports, one congressman was moved to observe: "I've never seen anyone who sells confusion as you do and gets so much money for it!"

The investigation had no immediate effect, but three years later, in the spring of 1966, one of the members of the congressional investigation staff, Rex Sparger, burst into headlines with the boast that he had successfully "rigged" the Nielsen ratings. Nielsen sued him, and in the ensuing court action some fascinating facts came to light.

It seems that some days prior to the prime-time telecast of a special program starring Carol Channing and produced by Ms. Channing's husband, Charles Lowe, some sixty residents of Ohio and Pennsylvania received letters from Sparger soliciting their comments on the commercials that were scheduled to appear in the program. Along with the letter went a cash payment of three dollars, with the promise that an additional five dollars would be sent to anyone who answered and returned the enclosed questionnaire in an envelope (also enclosed) which was addressed to a New York City post office box. The sixty recipients were Nielsen guinea pigs.

Obviously, the recipients couldn't watch the commercials if they didn't tune in to the program. If all sixty had had their curiosity piqued (or simply wanted the additional five dollars), the total tune-in would account for between five and six rating points in the national Nielsen report.

Although Lowe said he never intended to artificially boost the rating, he admitted having paid Sparger four thousand dollars "simply to obtain an evaluation of the effectiveness of the program."

Because Sparger boasted that he had "kited" the ratings a number of times before without Nielsen's knowledge, the rating service brought suit against him. It was settled when Sparger withdrew his claim that he had gotten away with many cases of successful tampering. The fascinating question is how Sparger got the names of the supposedly confidential list of Nielsen subjects. At one point, it was suggested that it was as simple as his following a Nielsen field man on his rounds. The rating-service executives alleged that he had stolen the list from the field man's automobile. In the settlement, Sparger admitted only that he had obtained the names by "improper or illegal means." Meanwhile, the air was filled with rumors. Nielsen did not reply to a *Los Angeles Times* story that quoted an unnamed network vice-president as saying that his network knew the location of four hundred Nielsen homes. Nor did Nielsen bother to announce whether the sixty homes on its Ohio-Pennsylvania list continued to report as usual.

4

The Networks and the Television Stations

"Certainly it takes more work for a station which does not rely on a network. It is far easier to patch in the network and have a full day and night's programming. I do not blame stations for preferring that course of life. I would myself. In fact, we try out best to make this an attractive way of life."
—Frank Stanton, president of CBS, before the Senate Committee on
Interstate and Foreign Commerce in 1954

The networks alone do not make up the television world. There are many other elements, the most noticeable of which are stations, program producers, and advertisers. Shouldn't they bear equal responsibility for the conduct of the industry and for what appears on America's television screens? Each network has two hundred station affiliates, some of which are owned by powerful companies like Westinghouse, General Tire, and the nation's largest newspaper and magazine publishing chains. The ranks of the television-program producers include all the major motion-picture companies, some of which are backed by mammoth conglomerates like Gulf and Western, Warner Communications, and Transamerica Corporation. The advertisers comprise all of America's corporate giants, some of the largest and most powerful concentrations of capital in the world. Can it be that all of these parties, when they do business with a network, are dominated by the network?

Since the stations are a network's bedrock, let's first examine the affiliate relationship. Initially, the association rested on a contract whereby the network agreed to act as agent or trustee for the station in selling the station's time to advertisers, and the station agreed to telecast whatever programs the network sent to it during specified hours each day.

The relationship between the networks and their affiliated stations has been changing throughout television history. The Federal Communications Commission, which licenses all stations, limits any single owner to five VHF transmitters. As a result, fifteen of the most powerful and prosperous stations in the country are owned and operated by the three networks. All three chains own stations in New York, Los Angeles, and Chicago, the three biggest cities. CBS fills out its quota with the fourth largest market, Philadelphia, and St. Louis (twelfth). ABC owns the sixth and seventh largest, Detroit and San Francisco. NBC has the eighth and ninth, Cleveland and Washington. The CBS- and ABC-owned stations reach 22.8 percent and the NBC-owned stations reach 21.9 percent of all television homes in the United States.

Television stations obtain their revenue by selling their sole commodity, time, to advertisers. Buoyed by the strength of their owned and operated stations, and pursuing practices they had established in radio, the networks emerged as national sales agents for the stations with whom they contracted as affiliates. And they were exactly that, agents or brokers who arranged with national advertisers for nationwide television

exposure. In the beginning, the networks did not control programming other than news, sports, and public-service productions. The advertiser owned his program; most often he
produced it himself or through his advertising agency. He
sought to make sure that he could buy time and get the program with which he wanted to be identified on the stations he
wanted. The network did this for the advertiser by clearing
with the station and collecting from the advertiser an amount
of money based on what the station charged for its time. The
network collected a handsome percentage of the fee for its services, and a goodly sum went to the American Telephone and
Telegraph Company for the use of its lines. The station owner
wound up with about 30 percent of the amount he would ask
from a local advertiser if he was selling the time on his own,
but he didn't complain. After all, he got a good show without
having either to produce or pay for it. He didn't have to send
salesmen out to solicit advertising; he simply had to press a
button.

By 1959, when television was about twelve years old, the
networks were well into the process of removing the advertiser
from any position of power in these dealings. They would no
longer permit sponsors to own or control shows, and they
squelched any further notion that an advertiser had about his
"franchise" or his right to any time period: the networks produced or bought the programs. They still sold sponsorship
rights to whole series, charging the buyer separately for the
show and for time based on the aggregate of station rates, so
matters stayed on an even keel insofar as the stations were concerned. The only difference was that now the network was furnishing the broadcaster a commodity as well as a sales service.

Recently the networks have refined the sales operation and

increased their profit at the expense of the broadcaster by ceasing to sell shows or segments to a sponsor. A network sells commercial announcements of thirty or sixty seconds' duration, and its charges bear no relation to the affiliated stations' rate cards. Advertisers pay, as we have seen, on the basis of dollars-per-thousand-viewers, and as a successful show climbs in the ratings the price of announcements increases accordingly. The stations and the producer get the glory while the network gets the money. The network is no longer the station's agent; it is the station's supplier. It is in a position to drive a hard bargain, and it does.

Until fifteen years ago, the affiliation contract required the station to take all network offerings during favored time segments. This period of mandatory clearance, which was called option time because the affiliate "optioned" its time during such intervals to the network, was abolished by an FCC order in the mid-sixties so that affiliated stations could use the freed time for nonnetwork programming, an expectation that proved illusory.

Network programming is sent to the affiliates electronically from network headquarters or "master control." There is an alternate source of programming, delivered manually on a station-by-station basis, known as "syndication." Syndication can encompass all forms of programming except that which is done live, that is, performances that are broadcast while being performed.

In television's earlier days there was considerable "live" broadcasting. Some programming was on film, but the remainder was seen while it was actually performed. With the perfection of color tape, live programs have disappeared from prime-time schedules, except for certain fast-breaking news and sports events. While ordinary newscasts are done live, the only part of the show that is not usually prerecorded is the newscaster himself, who watches the camera and reads script; the visual parts of the normal newscast are either filmed or taped on location prior to the broadcast. In any event, "live action" is now extremely rare during prime time.

The use of tape or film has a number of advantages over the old-fashioned live show. It can be cut and edited to remove mistakes, it can be reduced to exactly the required running time, it can be played at the same "clock time" in each of the four time zones of the country (in the early days of television, an eight o'clock show originating in the East would be seen at five o'clock on the West Coast). Most important, the filmed or taped program can be run and rerun at later dates, giving it what the trade calls residual value. Although the three networks and occasional separate sports and news hookups must use the interconnected cable or microwave relay for "simultaneous network telecast," the almost universal use of tape and film for entertainment programs has, to a large extent, made simultaneous transmission unnecessary.

Independent stations that are not affiliated with any network (and this includes many UHFs as well as the independent VHFs in the fifteen cities we have already referred to) get their staple programming in the form of directly delivered film and tape. The independent station, not being connected with any other, must rely on syndication, except for the live shows it can afford to produce for purely local consumption.

There are three types of syndicated programming. There is "first-run" programming, which is produced specifically for syndication. It includes talk shows like those presided over by Merv Griffin and Mike Douglas, some game strips, and the half-hour programming created for the "prime time access period." (In the early 1970s the Federal Communications Commission decreed that on weeknights the affiliated stations in the fifty largest cities could not accept more than three hours of network programming in prime-time, except for news; since most of these stations ran news at 7:00 P.M., this left the half-hour starting at 7:30 P.M. [Eastern Time] for syndicated or local shows, a segment of the day known as the prime-time access period.)

The bulk of syndicated programming is "off-network" shows. These are network series that won large audiences and stayed on the network long enough (usually four or five years or more) so that there were sufficient episodes to be "stripped."

The third form of syndicated programming consists of old movies that were made for theaters and are now sold for television viewing. They may or may not have previously run on one of the networks.

Ever since the FCC ruled that it is illegal for a station to option its time to a network, it has been possible for an affiliated station to substitute a syndicated program or series it might want for an undesirable network show. But any such independence on the part of an affiliate makes a network extremely unhappy. After all, the network has sold the advertiser on nationwide coverage, it has charged him on the basis of a dollar cost for each thousand viewers, and the subtraction of viewers is financially damaging to it. Most useful to the network is the economic threat inherent in the fact that network affiliation is of tremendous monetary value to a television station. Not only is there a steady stream of expensively produced programming geared to attract the largest part of the most desirable mass audience, not only are there ready-made national sponsors who have already bought and paid for the station's time, but there is freedom from the predicament of trying to program on a local basis with an ever-dwindling supply of new material. Because of attractive network programming the independent station that is trying to compete with the affiliate finds its audience diminishing, and as its audience diminishes it must cut its time charges. With less money coming in, the station has less to spend on programming. And as this circle works its way round and round, the independent station finds itself relegated to a second-rate position in the market.

The contrast, which applies not only to struggling UHF stations but to nonnetwork VHF stations as well, is clearest during prime time, when the sets-in-use figure jumps from 30 percent to 60 percent. The advertising-agency account executive measures what he can spend for an announcement by the number of desired viewers that his commercial will reach. This in turn depends on the popularity of the program in which his announcement is placed or to which it is adjacent. With the network's monopoly of "attractive" air time, the independent stations simply cannot find programming that can compete.

Many metropolitan stations today don't bother to publish a "rate card," the traditional price list prepared for the buyers and the advertising agencies. This is because they now sell on a cost-per-viewer basis. The station estimates its rating and the buyer pays accordingly; if the program fails to fulfill the station's guess, the advertiser gets a "make-good"—that is, the station owes him the difference in rating points and makes it up to him with additional announcements without further charge. But where the old-fashioned rate-card is still published, it shows dramatically the dollar value of network affiliation. In Los Angeles, for example, the highest rate for a 30-second announcement in 1976 on the ABC-owned station was $5,000;

on the CBS-owned station it was $5,250; and on the NBC-owned station it was $6,000. The rates for the equivalent spot on the four nonnetwork VHF stations were $500, $600, and two at $400. In New York, the NBC-owned station's 30-second prime-time spot was listed at $10,000, with independent VHF station WPIX at $865, and independent WOR at $600. In Chicago, where there is only one independent VHF, WGN-TV, the equivalent listed rate was $1,250 in contrast to the $5,400 of the NBC station.

Clearly, a network affiliation represents tremendous dollar value for a television station; the network's power over its affiliates can be judged accordingly. There are many illustrations of this but perhaps none so dramatic as the historic confrontation between NBC and the giant Westinghouse Corporation. The case began twenty years ago and involved a decade of legal maneuvers, including a decision by the United States Supreme Court.

The problem was the logical consequence of the FCC rule stating that no one company can own more than five VHF television stations. NBC had assumed that there was nothing to prevent it from owning and operating its stations in any five markets it chose. Naturally it chose the big ones. (There is more money to be made in the larger markets because there are more viewers, and it doesn't cost any more for equipment to build the station or power or personnel to run it.) Prior to 1956, NBC owned VHF television stations in New York, Los Angeles, Chicago, Cleveland, and Washington. New York, Los Angeles, and Chicago were the three largest cities in America. The next largest city after Chicago is Philadelphia. The NBC affiliate in Philadelphia was owned and operated by the Westinghouse Broadcasting Corporation. Westinghouse had owned the NBC radio affiliate for many years, but not until 1953 did it acquire the television station from the Philco Corporation, for $8.5 million. Westinghouse and Philco had agreed that $5 million of the sum was the value of the affiliation with NBC at that time. Westinghouse executives later testified that the revenues in 1953 and 1954 more than justified this allocation.

In 1955, NBC decided to exchange its Cleveland station for the more profitable Philadelphia station. The network proposed that Westinghouse give up Philadelphia and take over Cleveland, and receive a $3 million payment as a sort of consolation prize. Westinghouse resisted this proposition, but NBC made it clear that it had previously been offered the opportunity to acquire another Philadelphia station and that it would prefer the Westinghouse outlet. The Westinghouse people later told the FCC that the acquisition by NBC of its own radio and television stations in Philadelphia would, of course, mean the end of NBC affiliation for the Westinghouse stations and the loss of that part of the $8.5 million purchase price designated as the value of the affiliation. The element of coercion was plain. As the chief of the FCC's Broadcast Bureau later said, "The vital force of a major network affiliation hung constantly over these negotiations, exerting its own pressure without ever expressly coming to the forefront." The Westinghouse people were disturbed by what their president described as a "muscling job," but the economic consequences from the loss of network affiliation were such that even this powerful company believed that submission would be the better part of valor.

The Westinghouse president later testified that "much as Westinghouse disliked the situation they found themselves in, there was not much they could do except to get the best deal they could from NBC and since it was clear that Philadelphia was NBC's real objective it was decided to bargain for the best possible advantages in exchange for Cleveland." Westinghouse accordingly joined with NBC in asking the FCC to approve the swap. Although two of the commissioners said they were bothered by the glaring circumstance that "the expiration of the NBC affiliation agreement triggered the negotiations which led to the transfer," the others noted that Westinghouse had said it was exercising a prudent business judgment, and the FCC gave its approval.

So NBC took over Philadelphia and Westinghouse was relegated to Cleveland. There were stirrings, however, within the Department of Justice, and after little more than a year had passed, the government filed a complaint against NBC asking that the exchange agreement be voided because it was in violation of the Sherman Anti-Trust Act. The attorney general charged that the network had conspired to grab ownership of stations in five of the eight largest cities in the country "by the unlawful use of the power of the Defendant NBC, as a network, to grant or withhold from nonnetwork station owners, NBC network affiliation for their television stations."

The case wound its way to the Supreme Court, the lawyers debating whether or not the courts could hear an antitrust case after an FCC decision. The high tribunal held that the federal courts certainly could go into this question despite the FCC action, and sent the case back for the taking of evidence. By this time NBC had had enough. The network was understandably wary of any judicial investigation of its monopoly and how it was using it. NBC entered into a consent decree whereby it agreed to sell the Philadelphia outlet after an allotted number of years and pick up its fifth station somewhere else. Even so, it wasn't until 1965 that NBC withdrew its attempt to acquire a station in Boston or San Francisco, and reversed the swap, moving back to Cleveland. By this time, according to the experts, the Philadelphia affiliation value had increased from $5 million to $20 million, and it probably carries from two to four times that value today.

When loss of network affiliation can induce a giant corporation such as Westinghouse to abandon the nation's fourth-largest television market rather than remain there without network affiliation, the pressure that networks can bring to bear upon affiliates in clearing programs becomes self-evident.

However much a local affiliate might prefer to exercise independent judgment in selecting competitive programs over network fare, the station cannot afford network disfavor, which could place its affiliation in jeopardy. There is a maxim in the industry that the courage of a network-affiliated station is shown in inverse ratio to the number of stations in the market. For example, in a city with only two broadcasters both can be extremely brave, for the network has no place to go. In a three-station market, courage will be shown only by the affiliate of the lowest ranking of the three networks, because the other two stations are afraid that they might be relegated to the bottom spot. In any city where there are four VHF stations nobody shows any courage, because fear of losing the affiliation to the hungry independent is a constant. (This would not apply to New York, Los Angeles, and Chicago, because all of the affiliates in those cities are owned and operated by the networks, and by definition the owned-and-operated station doesn't do anything that its owner doesn't want it to do.)

The cost of producing a syndicated program or series must approach that of producing a prime-time network show, if the two are to compete for the audience on equal terms. In order to recoup that amount of money the syndicator must be able to sell his show to stations in all the major cities at the high price that is available only if the program runs in prime time. If the affiliated stations are afraid to preempt in prime time, the syndicated show cannot survive. There simply are not enough nonnetwork stations able to pay for entertainment of a quality to compete with that which runs on the networks.

The network-inspired restraint on program preemption by their affiliates has developed simultaneously with a steady growth in the use of station time by the networks. In 1960 the three national networks programmed 434 half-hours weekly on a combined regularly scheduled basis. By 1976 that figure had climbed to 540, virtually all of which were cleared by affiliates. This increase occurred despite the advent, in the fall of 1971, of the prime-time access rule, which gave twenty-one half-hours back to the stations. As a matter of fact, from 1972 to 1976, network programming grew by 46.5 half-hour units per week.

Most damaging to other elements of the industry has been the networks' tireless appropriation of prime time, much of which had been accomplished by the early 1960s. Before then the networks used from 8:00 P.M. to 10:30 P.M. (Eastern Time), which left available 7:00 to 8:00, and 10:30 to 11:00. During the 1950s these time periods were usually programmed with first-run syndicated half-hour shows; during those years an average of thirty new syndicated half-hour series were made for prime time. But as the networks established themselves in these time slots, the producers of syndicated programming dropped out of business, one by one, until by the end of the 1960s there were literally no first-run syndicated programs being produced for the attractive evening hours. There was no way, as we have seen, for the producers to get enough money from the limited number of viable independent stations to pay production costs.

The elimination of the first-run syndication business had a domino effect that redounded further to the networks' benefit. By removing a source of quality programming it lowered the independent stations on the competitive scale. Even the few prosperous nonnetwork VHF stations in the largest cities were compelled to adopt strip programming in prime time, trying without much success to compete with their network peers by offering daily sets of off-network repeats, game shows, and low-budget talk shows. (Talk shows prosper by sufferance of the talent unions who have ruled that guest stars are essentially interviewees, and are, therefore, allowed to appear at the low union minimum rather than at their customary high fee.)

The FCC and committees of both houses of Congress expressed concern about the demise of prime-time syndication. As far back as 1956 they had been warned about what would happen. Richard M. Moore, at that time manager of KTTV, an independent VHF station in Los Angeles, testified that "access to the public's most convenient viewing hours is effectively barred by the networks to local and nonnetwork program sources and local and nonnetwork advertisers; and the choice of what the American public may see during these most convenient hours is effectively determined by unilateral decisions at the network headquarters in New York." He accurately predicted that first-run syndicated programming would "shrink and disappear, and independent television stations like KTTV will be unable to obtain access to the few high-quality films that may still be produced. If independent stations cannot obtain access to such programs, the stations' potential for service to their communities will be destroyed."

Congressional committees came and went. The FCC's Network Study Group investigated the problem for eight years, much of which time was spent taking testimony. The first concrete step was taken in 1971 when the FCC adopted the prime-time access rule. In order to truly encourage alternative program sources, the commission prohibited the use of off-network reruns during the new access period, such provision to go into effect in 1972. (The rule was later amended to free Sundays from its operation.) The new rule opened up a half-hour on each of six nights, because most affiliates utilized the news exception. With three networks this looked like space for eighteen new half-hour weekly series—a step in the right direction.

However, there were many problems. In the first place, one purpose of the rule was to free the producers of the new shows from the network stranglehold. As a matter of practical financing, no syndicated show that carries a respectably high price tag can succeed unless it is sold in New York and Los Angeles. As we have seen, however, because they had been unable to get this type of series for over fifteen years, the independent stations in New York and Los Angeles had developed the practice of stripping. Suddenly faced with the prospect of not having to meet network competition from 7:30 to 8:00 P.M., and not being subject to the prohibition against off-network reruns during that half-hour, the independent stations weren't about to change this habit. The consequence was that the reborn producer found himself unable to market his series unless he got a deal from the network stations in the top two cities. These, of course, are owned and operated by the networks themselves. So the producer couldn't even get started with his show without the okay of one of the networks, albeit a different branch of the company from the one he used to see.

In the second place, by making the access period the same

on every night and on every network, the FCC inadvertently created a low-budget-show ghetto. It was assumed that because a program is syndicated it must cost less to produce than one that is sent over network transmission, presumably because of higher distribution expense. While there is some truth in this, the difference is exaggerated in many an expert mind, and no account is taken of production-cost savings. In any event, as the new arrangement was conceived by the FCC, access programs would compete only against other access programs, not against network fare. They have, therefore, tended to consist mainly of game shows, nature or "animal" shows, and a few modest variety shows. There was no need for this to happen. The period could have been decreed one that must differ from network to network. It could have been placed at different times and perhaps on different days, maybe not always a half-hour in length. In this way the syndicated and local programs would compete with network shows, as they did in the earlier days of television, often with marked success, thus putting a premium on creativity and encouraging the imaginative exercise of American production talent.

Third, the 7:30 to 8:00 P.M. time period is the most difficult for new programming. Since TV sets are often controlled by children at this hour, an attempt is made to produce a show that a child will prefer but that is not so unbearable that Mommy won't stay in the room to watch it ("Mommy" is presumably a woman between the ages of eighteen and forty-nine). This is called "bi-modal" or "kidult" programming, the distinguishing features of which are sentimentality and blandness.

The selection of the 7:30 time period was actually worked out by the networks. Assuming that the half-hour must be either at the beginning or end of prime time, they preferred to give up 7:30 to 8:00 rather than 10:30 to 11:00, because the earlier slot had traditionally been more difficult to sell. No one network dared let a rival start networking first, on the theory that this would give it an unbeatable head start (the flow-of-audience theory), but once all three had agreed to make it 7:30, the matter was settled.

Although Don McGannon, president of the Westinghouse stations, had been agitating for the new rule for some time before 1971, it was believed that FCC didn't act until it was pretty well satisfied that the networks were not really opposed to the rule. They had had a relatively slow year for sales in 1970, and 7:30 to 8:00 had been especially difficult. Also the ban on cigarette commercials, which was about to go into effect, would account for about the same amount of commercial time that the rule would take away from the networks' inventory. One of the networks, ABC, favored Prime-Time Access from the beginning. NBC at first opposed it, then did a switch and dropped its obstruction. Only CBS consistently opposed it, but even CBS appeared to back down when it announced that, despite its objection to the rule, there should be no change until two years later.

Television stations are themselves little monopolies. The control of an exclusive VHF franchise in any American city is a prize of great value. The broadcaster, however, doesn't own the right to operate a station. It is licensed to him by the people of the United States acting through the FCC, and the license must be renewed every three years. The kind-hearted members of the FCC, however, have consistently renewed television station licenses, their only refusals being for a repeated violation of technical rules resulting in the transmission of unacceptable signals. That's why we read of sales of TV stations in major cities going as high as thirty times annual earnings. What is really being sold is a monopoly that the seller doesn't legally own but which is treated as though he does.

The one instance of a station's being forced off the air without technical violations is the famous case of Boston's Channel 5. This was no failure to renew, since no license had ever been granted. The publisher of the *Boston Herald-Traveler* was operating the station on a temporary permit, which was contested by two other applicants. The litigation lasted seventeen years, the longest regulatory case in American history. Some of the evidence had to do with the propriety of a controversial off-the-record lunch that the president of the operating company had with the chairman of the FCC, which is why Sterling Quinlan entitled his book about the case *The Hundred Million Dollar Lunch.* The book answers in detail the question "How do you blow one hundred million dollars, seventeen years of legal wrangling, two million dollars in legal expenses, and wind up losing your station and your newspaper?" (The station had been making more money than the newspaper lost, so three months after the station's demise the *Herald* joined it in the graveyard.)

A more typical case involved the license renewal for WPIX-TV, the New York City independent station associated with the *New York Daily News.* This case occupied the FCC for nine years. WPIX's license had been challenged in 1969 on grounds of alleged distortion of the news in televised reports. During the 1968 anti-Soviet uprising in Czechoslovakia, the station had credited news reports to cities where the action was rather than where the reporter was broadcasting. It was also alleged that WPIX had filmed a tank in Fort Belvoir, Virginia, as if it were in Vietnam's central highlands, and that the station had superimposed the legend "via satellite" over news film that had been delivered by express. The challengers believed that such actions constituted efforts to "deceive station viewers" and were "an attempt to hype news ratings—it was simply a matter of greed." They pointed out that when the matter had been brought to the attention of the president and general manager of the station, his response was to fire the reporter who told him about it.

In June 1978 the FCC renewed the WPIX license. The vote was four to three. The majority did not go along with their administrative law judge, who had taken the position that to be concerned with falsification and misrepresentation of the news would be a violation of the station's First Amendment rights, but it did say that news distortion and inadequate supervision did not involve misdeeds of sufficient importance to warrant denial of renewal. It is interesting to note that even had the decision gone the other way WPIX would have already enjoyed nine years of extremely profitable operation after the time of challenge, and its certain subsequent appeal to the courts would have involved more time, perhaps even approaching the seventeen years that the Boston station managed after the time of its original application.

As we have noted, in the early days of television the networks acted as a clearinghouse and collected the station's share of the sponsor's payment on its behalf. The network and the station jointly agreed on what the share should be, based on the station's regularly charged rates. "We are partners in a joint venture," was the way NBC president Robert Sarnoff put it.

Later, when the networks took control of program production, they charged the advertiser separately for "time and talent," "talent" meaning production, and the "time" charge being based on the aggregate of what the stations would get, in addition to miscellaneous expenses like line charges and overhead. The network, in other words, was still considered a conduit between the advertiser and the stations. If, then, the actual expense of operating the network went up, it followed that this expense would be taken out of the payments to the local stations. In 1969 when A.T.&T. raised its charges to the networks for long-distance transmission of programs, the cost increase was passed on to the affiliates in the form of an immediate decrease in their network compensation rates. After all, a clearinghouse took no risk, it just worked the nuts and bolts.

Today the system has changed. The networks sell 30- to 60-second announcements, not programs that cover a half-hour or an hour of desirable time. Experts argue about the reasons for the change. Under the old system advertisers benefited from the identification with a popular entertainment. The very name was a boon to the sponsors of the "Texaco Star Theater," the "Firestone Hour," the "Kraft Music Hall," the "Kaiser Aluminum Hour," and the "Lucky Strike Hit Parade." When the advertiser lost the opportunity to coproduce or buy his chosen show, and when he could no longer "own" his pet time period, much of his advantage disappeared. Rising costs may also have had something to do with the change; between 1960 and 1976, the average cost to produce a half-hour prime-time series episode jumped by about 237 percent from $49,000 to $165,000, and the cost of a 30-second prime-time network announcement increased by 153 percent, which may have been somewhat higher than the normal rate of inflation. Also, advertisers said that they had come to realize that they got more bang-for-a-buck out of a lot of short announcements spread over the dial than out of a few longer but more concentrated commercials. They said that the quickie plugs were "more cost effective."

Whether or not these Madison Avenue conclusions were rationalizations to support a new plan that the networks found most attractive for themselves, it does seem true that some ad-agency account executives welcomed the change because it absolved them of the responsibility of making rough decisions. When an advertiser fully sponsored a series, he put all his eggs in one basket, and woe to the agency genius who suggested what turned out to be a bad basket. The new system took a lot of relieved admen off the spot.

The networks were characteristically quick on the uptake. They were in full control of the programming, the time, and the stations. They had eliminated the roles formerly played by advertisers and agencies. They no longer had to "represent" or be "partners" with stations. The price of announcements was geared to the number of viewers; if a show increased in popularity, the advertiser would pay more—and the network could keep the difference. There is a set station-rate per announcement, so there is no obligation to increase payment to the stations. The money the network pays the station for carrying a show no longer has to be related to what the advertiser pays; it can simply be one of the network's business expenses.

Today the network sets the figure it will use in calculating the payment for each commercial announcement carried by the affiliate. Networks pay nothing for any commercial minutes that are not sold. The station receives less compensation even though the overall program time taken by the network remains the same.

This change was immediately reflected in network profit figures. Total network income in 1971 was $53.7 million. By 1972 it had leapt to $110.9 million, a 107 percent increase. By 1973 it was $184.8 million, a jump of 67 percent. By 1974, profits reached the $200 million mark, and they were recorded at $208.5 million in 1975. By 1976 the figure was $295.6 million, up 42 percent, and in 1977, $406.1 million, a 37 percent rise.

From the network's point of view, the process has been simplified. If a series is not a ratings success, the network drops it. If it is a hit, the money rolls in and the network keeps the money. If the show becomes a favorite it stays on for a number of years. The network pays a little more money to the producer each year under the "escalation" clause in the production contract—about 5 percent. The network may have to sweeten the fee paid to the star who threatens to break his contract (and hence ruin the show) unless he gets more money, but in the overall production cost this boosts the total by only a few percentage points. The network pays the affiliated stations no more for the time; the stations must be content with the fact that a hit show improves their ratings and raises the value of commercial announcements that are adjacent to the network program or are available during the half-hourly station breaks. But the advertiser will have to pay the network price increases commensurate with the increase in the size of the audience.

The Westinghouse stations, in their petition to the FCC, alleged that a large portion of the newly accumulated network wealth has accrued at the expense of the affiliates. During the ten years in which the networks' income rose from $92 million to $225 million, a 143 percent increase, the total compensation they paid their affiliates fell 2.3 percent, a $6 million drop. This looks more startling when you see that in 1974 the networks gave the stations less than 14 percent of the broadcasters' revenue, whereas in 1964 the figure was more than 23 percent.

The affiliated stations have other complaints. They allege that their own networks are now competing with them in selling commercials to national advertisers for regional coverage by undercutting the price. They claim this happens because the networks have reduced their compensation and have been accepting orders for 30-second messages instead of insisting on the 1-minute minimum. (Between 1967 and 1974, the number of commercial minutes available for sale by the networks increased from 100,000 to 105,600, while the number of available announcements jumped from 103,000 to 170,400.)

In addition to encroachments upon time previously allotted for station use, the networks have recently been increasing the amount of commercial time sold by them during prime-time programs. The National Association of Broadcasters, through its Code of Fair Practice, has established that the proper amount of time for commercial announcements during prime-time should be six minutes per hour. A few years ago the networks added another minute per hour for movies because of what they styled the "high cost of theatrical features." During the past one or two years they have applied this rule to practically every prime-time program longer than one hour. This includes miniseries, movies made for television, and even the longer versions of regular series episodes.

Fearing that this trend would continue, President Donald McGannon of Westinghouse notified the three networks on January 14, 1978, that the Westinghouse stations (two affiliated with CBS, two with NBC, and one with ABC) would refuse to run any commercial announcements that exceeded the levels which existed on January 1, 1978, and would replace them with public-service or public-affairs announcements. He said that he was afraid that there would soon be four commercial minutes instead of three in each prime-time half-hour, which would increase the total network income by $570 million per year, a figure based on the estimate that the 1977 network revenues were $3.422 billion, of which prime time represents about half.

CBS's "Saturday Night Movie" scheduled for May 20, 1978, was *Hannie Calder*. Carrying out his threat, McGannon ordered the Westinghouse stations to delete one of the commercial announcements and substitute a public-service announcement. CBS retaliated by refusing to send *Hannie Calder* to its two Westinghouse affiliates. Westinghouse stated that they believed the amount of non-program time being used by CBS was excessive. "The two-hour period from 9:00 to 11:00 P.M. was formatted by CBS to include 14 minutes of network commercial time and 2 minutes of local commercial time within a 93-minute movie which was followed by 11 consecutive minutes of promotional announcements for other CBS programs. We concluded this amount of non-program time was excessive and contrary to the public interest." Mr. McGannon later said that the eleven minutes of promotional material raised a "philosophical question" inasmuch as such material is "akin in nature to commercials themselves." To reduce the entertainment portion of a two-hour prime-time program to an hour and thirty-three minutes certainly makes TV watching that much less attractive, while diluting the value of what the station has to sell to the individual advertiser.

Many affiliated stations feel that the present system makes it impossible for them to carry out properly their responsibilities as license holders. The FCC has consistently said that the local station is ultimately responsible for what goes out over the air; the station cannot defer responsibility to the network or any other entity, such as an advertiser. Under the law the station licensee is required to program "in the public interest," with regard for the special needs and desires of the local community. What may be suitable in New York or Los Angeles might be unacceptable in other cities. Yet there is little chance to exercise this policy as long as the networks supply the programming. Because the affiliated stations do not participate in network decisions concerning programs, and because those same stations do not review most of the shows prior to broadcast, it is practically impossible for the affiliates to carry out the localism rule.

The network often receives a program only a day or two before it is aired. Clearly there is little time for affiliates to obtain and schedule substitute programming in the event they decide against the network show. But there is no reason why programs must be delivered at the last minute. Most programs are not so topical that a slight increase in the time between production and exhibition is impractical. It may well be that the networks wish to avoid giving the affiliates the right to preview program episodes, fearing that this might lead to additional preemptions.

Everett C. Parker, director of the Office of Communications of the United Church of Christ, writing in the *New York Times* on September 25, 1977, pointed out that under the law "the individual station licensee is still the trustee of the frequency it occupies, still responsible for everything that goes on the air." This led him to the conclusion that "it was never the intention of the Congress to have programming become the monopoly of three gigantic national corporations that can force their product on local stations willy-nilly with economic annihilation as the alternative; nor to have virtually all programs originate in Hollywood or New York with the talent of the rest of the nation excluded; nor to have prime-time programs aimed only at the limited audience of people between 18 and 49, as the networks now do, excluding the rest. Today the average network-affiliated television station has no control over 65 percent of its programs. At best, it can only say yes or no to the network; it has little influence on network decisions."

5

The Networks
and the Producers

"You know and we know, as practical men, that the question of justice arises only between parties equal in strength, and that the strong do what they can, and the weak submit."

—Thucydides, *History of the Peloponnesian War*

There was a time when an independent creator could produce and sell television programs in a free and open market. There were a large number of potential customers for a television series. A producer could sell it to any one of dozens of national advertisers for network exposure, or he could originate it in syndication by direct sale to stations or to regional or local sponsors. There were numerous sellers as well as many buyers, so bargaining was on an even keel. The parties would negotiate what both agreed was a fair price for the right to broadcast. The show would still be owned by its producer, and after its run was over, what he did with it by way of further use was his business.

As we have seen, the syndication of new prime-time series gradually diminished, concurrent with the networks' extension of their nightly coverage from 7:30 straight through to 11:00.

The last year that there were as many as thirty first-run prime-time syndicated series was 1956; by 1957 there were twenty; in 1959 there were fifteen; ten in 1960; three in 1963; and the last one (until Prime-Time Access) died in 1965.

The producer who sold to national advertisers for a network run encountered his first major obstacles in 1955. Because the network retained the right to approve material it disseminated, the advertiser would buy the program from a producer "subject to network approval." This would have created no problems were it not for the fact that at that time the network also went into the program-production business and competed with the very producer who was seeking approval. It was not unusual for the network to find it was less likely to approve the offering of an outside producer rather than a program that it owned or in which it had a substantial interest.

Loud were the howls of producers who found that after mastering the Scylla of selling to a sponsor, they then faced the Charybdis of a sale to a network. Many production companies quit or concentrated on the relatively simple business of making theatrical movies. But a more resilient group adapted to the new climate. At first they made quiet deals with network spokesmen, often agreeing to cut the network in on any profits that might be forthcoming from foreign sales and postnetwork reruns. This practice was not called bribery; it was characterized as payment to the network for taking a risk, or payment to the network in return for creative suggestions and advice.

The networks' next step was to remove the advertiser from the equation entirely and require the producer to deal directly with them, the logical progression from those furtive side-bar deals. At about the time network executives were trying to figure out how to announce and institute this move most discreetly, the 1959 quiz scandals broke. For months, "live action" shows, one on CBS called "The Sixty-Four Thousand Dollar Question" (later supplemented by the "Sixty-Four Thousand Dollar Challenge"), and one on NBC called "Twenty-One," had dominated the Nielsen ratings. Unprecedented numbers of viewers were transfixed by the spectacle of a contestant in an isolation booth, whose superhuman brain was apparently stuffed with miscellaneous esoterica and who invariably answered the most baffling questions just before the buzzer signaled his elimination.

The bubble burst when several of the winners of $64,000 and $100,000 confessed that the shows were staged and scripted entertainments rather than legitimate tests. According to newspaper editorials the American public was insulted. There were indignant speeches in both houses of Congress, and a highly publicized congressional investigation was undertaken.

There were some who called this the networks' darkest hour, but they underestimated the ingenuity of the great American communicator. CBS's and NBC's darkest hour became their finest hour. They turned defeat into victory, and at the same time solved that pressing problem of program control.

Frank Stanton, president of CBS, was the spokesman. The network, he said, was just as angry as the American people, and for the same reason. It had been deceived. The quiz shows had been performed in their studios and broadcast over their air, but the network did not produce them. They were made by outsiders called independent producers and had been brought in by advertisers. The network had no control and didn't know what was going on, and if it had, it would have stopped it. He said CBS should have been more vigilant, and then in a stirring and clever peroration said, "The American people hold the networks responsible for what appears on their schedules. From now on *we* will decide not only what is to appear, but *how*."

These shows had indeed been created and owned by outside firms, but they were broadcast from network studios on network premises, aided by the services of literally hundreds of network employees, many of whom were probably aware of what was going on. But it was more than a matter of liaison, especially in the case of CBS, for the "Sixty-Four Thousand Dollar Question" and the "Sixty-Four Thousand Dollar Challenge" had been owned and controlled by a man named Lou Cowan, who sold his interest, and who before exposure of the quiz show scandals had become president of the CBS television network.

Stanton was as good as his word, and he apparently expressed the feelings of all three networks. With few exceptions, from that time forward producers who had a prime-time series to sell would deal with a network. And though this sounds like three buyers, it meant, as we shall see, that for any individual series the producer would have but a single customer.

Producers weren't happy with the new arrangement, but most of them had learned to keep their complaints to themselves. Not so, however, David Susskind, who, speaking as head of his company, Talent Associates, testified before the FCC's Network Study Committee in June 1961. Susskind said that CBS told him that a show he brought to the network would have to be a CBS production.

> COUNSEL: It would have to be a CBS production?
> SUSSKIND: Yes, sir.
> COUNSEL: I see. Well, now, did they give you any reason why it had to be a CBS production?

SUSSKIND: They gave me a pretty good reason; they said: Take it or leave it.

COUNSEL: I see. Well, is this a new departure for you, sir?

SUSSKIND: Very new. You see, with the network, with the three network control of programming there are lots of new departures. It used to be . . . that you could sell to any one of fifty advertising agencies, any one of a hundred or a thousand advertisers or sponsors. Today you must sell to the network or you don't get on the air.

....

COUNSEL: Well, do you understand this to be a rule or policy of the networks now?

SUSSKIND: Well, I find it to be a rule where my own recent experience has been involved.

COUNSEL: I see.

SUSSKIND: That if I can't sell it to the network I can't get it on the air.

Finally, Mr. Susskind mentioned "three men" who, he said, "have a death grip on programming" in the television industry.

COUNSEL: What three men are you talking about, Mr. Susskind?

SUSSKIND: The heads of NBC, CBS, and ABC. It was formerly possible to sell a program to J. Walter Thompson on behalf of its clients, to McCann-Erickson on behalf of its clients, to B.B.D.&O. on behalf of its clients. The area of suggestion, the area of exciting sales, was infinitely larger than it is today. Today you must sell three men, because the networks control it with a viselike grip. If these three men and their minions reject your program conceptions, you simply don't get on the air. The fact that you could sell it to an advertiser or his agency is academic. This control, this vise, was born of the payola and quiz scandals, the answer to which was: "Well, we'll take over control," said the networks, "so that this sort of thing can't happen again."

The producer of a "special" may still go to an advertiser, for that is the one area where the old-fashioned concept of sponsorship remains. Even then the producer will probably wind up dealing with whatever network finds time in its schedule for the show. For all the rest of prime-time production—whether it be series, or movies made for television, or variety shows—the producer talks only to the network.

The problem the producer faces in dealing with a network is that he can't get as much money as it will cost him to make his show, and he generally gets pushed, pulled, hauled, and shoved at every turn of what is politely referred to as the bargaining process. Except in rare cases where he may be furnishing unusually desirable star talent, the producer has no power. But the star system is no longer a major factor in TV, especially since the networks have adopted the policy of signing star performers to contracts that require them to appear exclusively on that network. The networks may assign the star to the producer rather than the reverse. It is true that the producer may develop a series that becomes, or gives promise of becoming, very attractive to the network, but long before he reaches that point he will have been bound to a meager budget for many years. The network is too smart to place itself in a position of vulnerability that would tip the balance in the direction of bargaining equality.

Here is a typical example. A production company head learns from his vice-president assigned to find out such things that the program geniuses over at Network A are speculating about an hour action-adventure series for a year from next fall. He gets another of his vice-presidents to buy an option on a new book that sounds like what the network might want, the option being the right for a period of six months to offer the book as the basis for a TV series. (He makes a more elaborate deal with the author; it includes the right to make a pilot film and also a series, with complex provisions for fees and royalties in the event of success.) The producer takes the book to the network, where a program officer reads it and, let's say, likes it enough to risk five thousand dollars to "develop" it. At this stage development means that the network merely wants a competent television writer to prepare an outline of how he thinks the characters could be expanded and used in a series, plus a plot line for the pilot film, and perhaps some one-line ideas for future episodes. The producer says that the writer the network wants will charge more than five thousand dollars for that job. The network man tells the producer to make up the difference himself. They argue about it a bit, and finally agree to go ahead. "Have your business-affairs guys get in touch with mine," says the network man, and the meeting breaks up.

At this juncture, we should make two vital points. The first is that although the producer might have gone to any one of the three networks, he is bound now to just one. In theory he might approach one or both of the other chains if his first contact discards the project somewhere along the path of its development, but as a practical matter that seldom happens. Networks B and C assume that if the project isn't good enough for Network A, it is not good enough for them; it is "damaged goods" and they have plenty of their own fish to fry.

The second important point is that although the network has committed only five thousand dollars, nothing will be done, not even the five thousand will be spent, until the producer has agreed to a contract that in minute detail covers every possible contingency of his relationship with the network on this project over the next nine or ten years. Such contingencies include the cost of a pilot based on a still-unwritten outline, the cost of episodes of a series that could not go into production for at least another year, and the cost of episodes that might be made anywhere from two to six years in the future. All of the time and effort going into such negotiations may be wasted. If the network doesn't like the outline, the entire project can be aborted at the end of a few weeks. If so, it's unlikely that the five thousand dollars will be missed.

But the network won't take that chance. If they were enthusiastic about the potential of the outline, they might order a full script. They could then make a pilot, which might lead to a successful series. The network cannot afford to allow the producer to get into a position where at any stage of the process he would have something that the network really wants, unless the network has him legally bound to irrevocable terms. In the earliest stages the producer has nothing that the network cares very much about, not even an outline, while the network has everything the producer must have—the airwaves.

Thus, with the five thousand dollars as the trigger, the business-affairs representatives discuss figures that might eventually exceed sixteen thousand times that amount. They first discuss the price of the pilot film in the event that one is made. The producer complains that he can't possibly make a picture for the price that is offered. The network representative, inured to this plea, knows the pilot will cost more than the network says. He also knows that the producer will not stint on expenditure because the producer's primary interest is to make a pilot so attractive that the network will decide to order a series. The series is where he might make some money; there is no way that he can get rich out of a mere pilot film. So the network negotiator says no, to which the producer's representative assents.

The argument over the cost of series episodes, assuming the pilot should turn out well enough to justify this final step, will be similar. Once again the producer will protest that the money offered cannot pay his costs. The network representative realizes that this is true, but he also knows that this is the producer's customary risk. He is well aware of the fact that if the series should rate well and last for four or more years, the producer will be able to recoup his losses and, depending upon the degree of success and longevity of the series, make a substantial profit. The producer, in turn, knows the long odds in this gamble: the chances of going to series may be one in ten and the chances of such a series staying on the air more than three years are another one in ten; but what the hell, you can't make a hit if you don't get up to bat, and you don't get up to bat unless you play the network game. Besides, if the producer has another profitable business, like making theatrical movies, and he has to pay sizable income taxes, he can write off his television losses as a business expense and he can also get a tax advantage on any films he makes, an investment tax credit. So the public will pay part of the bill.

In the late seventies a vogue for miniseries and two-hour made-for-television movies introduced a type of programming that could not be standardized with respect to price and production techniques. Such shows might cost anywhere from $700,000 to $7,000,000, making it impossible to negotiate a price until after a script had been written. To induce the networks to permit such a delay, the producers were required to "freeze" the property in the event that the parties could not agree on the program production price. The producer could not take the program to either of the other two networks for from one to two years after the script was finished. This reinforcement of the one-customer syndrome preserved the network domination of the bargaining process.

Memoranda from network files, which were later subpoenaed by the Department of Justice in an antitrust case involving CBS and ABC, show that network executives know that they are paying producers less than must be spent in the production of programs. Thus, the CBS vice-president in charge of program negotiation signed a memo, dated February 22, 1967, directing the network to "estimate what CTN's [Columbia Television Network's] costs would be if CTN had to pay full production costs on all series." He wanted to "demonstrate the amount by which our program costs would escalate should we agree to pay the Majors [such as Twentieth Century-Fox, MGM, etc.] their full production costs instead of having them deficit finance series production." In a memo to his immediate superior, dated July 16, 1969, an ABC programming executive pointed out that ABC exploited its buying power by imposing low prices on suppliers of ninety-minute movies for television by engendering a feeling of pride and competition among the suppliers as a substitute for economic incentive. There were bitter overtones in his complaint that Screen Gems' top management was "intent on making a profit ... [and] has gone on record as being completely opposed to deficit financing in any way."

Although the networks retain their capacity to produce programs, they use it very sparingly today in the prime-time area. It costs a network as much to produce a program as it does anyone else, and there is no reason why the networks should make programs at a price higher than what they pay an outside producer. As long as producers stand in line to get the opportunity to lose money, in the hope that they'll hit the jackpot at the other end, there is no fiscal reason for the networks not to take advantage of it. Even the FCC has taken notice of what it calls "allegations that the unlimited network potential for producing their own entertainment programs can be used to obtain first-run programming at unreasonably low prices."

The producer and the network debate many more issues, always with the same result. They talk about the extent of time that various rights can be exercised, about how many repeats there can be in a year, about how many films will fill a minimum order. But one extremely sensitive subject will barely be touched on, and that is the matter of the network's options to renew the series for future years in the event that its first year proves successful. The network will ask for seven years of options and settle for no fewer than five. The network will offer an annual escalation in price of 3 percent. The producer will ask for 7 percent, and will settle for 5 percent. But the producer will not even suggest that perhaps there should be *no* options, that if the show scores well in the ratings so that advertisers increase the amount they pay for spots without damaging their "cost per thousand," it is his opportunity to profit and his right to ask for it. Options are assumed to be obligatory in every deal; this probably goes back to the days when networks sold shows, as distinct from time, to full or half-sponsors who became the beneficiaries of a series' rating success.

A related problem is a network's insistence that it alone, to the exclusion of its two rivals, must be the only outlet for any new series that evolves from the use of a character in the series under negotiation, which are called spin-offs. ("Rhoda" was a spin-off from the "Mary Tyler Moore Show"; sometimes there are spin-offs of spin-offs—"Maude" was a spin-off of "All in the Family" and "Good Times" was a spin-off of "Maude.") The problem for the producer, of course, is that even with a series successful enough to occasion a spin-off he is unable to obtain competitive bids and is bound to offer the spin-off to a single buyer.

In view of inflation, the 5 percent annual escalation in price often cannot cover increased costs. The effect of the low, price-fixed, long-term option is that if the show does not attract large enough audiences, it will not be renewed. The producer is left with heavy losses. If it is successful, it will be renewed, but at the standard, predetermined, below-cost fees. In the event of renewal, the series is worth dramatically more to the network (or in theory to another network) than the network's pre-fixed fee to the producer, because the amount the network charges the advertiser for the value of an announcement reflects the show's success. The high profits go to the network.

This point was brought home in a complaint by Lee Rich, producer of "The Waltons," the successful one-hour series on CBS. On September 23, 1974, the trade magazine *Broadcasting* reported that "Mr. Rich said he understands CBS is charging $100,000 for one minute of advertising on *The Waltons*—averaging a $600,000 intake for each one-hour program. 'Why, I don't get even half that sum to produce the show,' Mr. Rich complained."

Most producers, however, refrain from open criticism of their customers. When *The Nation* commissioned Anne Langman in 1956 to write a series of articles on the television industry, she had to report that "none of the independents I have talked with will allow me to quote them by name. Their position with the networks is already precarious and they fear that if they antagonize them further they will be unable to sell anything at all for network distribution."

On February 1, 1978, this rule of public silence was broken

by the senior vice-president for administration and production of Paramount Television, Art Frankel. Speaking in San Diego to the convention of the Association of Independent Television Stations, Frankel first pointedly disassociated his employer from what he was about to say. He then described the process of developing shows for networks as "akin to playing Russian roulette." He added: "Network programming executives are quite human, despite the fact that some have the tendency to view themselves as God-like." About the producer he said: "Caught between the upper pressure of steadily rising costs, especially in the guild and labor union areas, and the downward pressure of all three networks to hold the line on license fees, the supplier is fortunate indeed if he can come close to breaking even on a show in the first year or two. All of the leverage is with the network since the supplier is contractually bound to continue to deliver the show at the previously agreed-upon price."

In addition to its overweening power in the business area, the network dominates the producer with respect to program content. During the course of that stately minuet known as contract negotiation, the business-affairs contestants sometimes spar over who has what "creative controls." This dispute is frequently the most fruitless argument of all, since the exercise of any such rights depends upon the economic realities of the moment and has nothing to do with whatever may be codified on a piece of paper.

This is most obvious in the production of a pilot film or tape. If the representative of the network program department suggests an addition, deletion, or change in some part of the story, a change in characterization, action, stage business, or even casting or direction, or perhaps shooting location or method of scoring background music, the producer will go along. He may protest that the change will harm the story or cheapen the picture; he may scream that the network representative is irresponsible, spending the producer's money for him foolishly and wastefully. But he will go along, primarily because he knows that it is the network which decides whether this show will ever go to series, and the program representative will probably have something to say about that. His isn't the only pilot that is being made for this network; there are probably five or six available for each open time-period that may exist one year from the shooting dates. After all, the whole point of this costly exercise is to get a series on the air; there is no purpose in continuing with a show that the network won't like.

The same forces are in play to only a slightly lesser extent in the production of the series. The network can always decide not to renew a series, or simply cancel earlier on. Both parties recognize that the future of the show depends on its ability to attract a large, demographically "right" audience, which, because of the network's elaborate research techniques, the producer is in no position to oppose. Only when his series has achieved the status of the rare smash hit can the producer assert his creative independence. Until then he would agree with the late Speaker of the House, Sam Rayburn, who said, "The way to get along is to go along."

You will remember that CBS's Frank Stanton initiated this procedure in his righteously indignant declaration at the time of the quiz scandals: "From now on *we* will decide not only what is to appear, but *how.*" Less than four years later, his corporation was able to assure its stockholders that they as viewers could depend on the "continuing participation of the Network's programming officials at every stage of the creative process from the initial script to the final broadcast."

NBC and ABC have immodestly acknowledged similar control, and in the case of the latter, an internal memo disclosed an engaging frankness about one of the benefits of the policy. In 1965, ABC was considering the production of a series entitled "Blue Light" through its wholly owned subsidiary, Selmur Productions, but after analyzing the risk of having to deficit finance the series, ABC contracted with Twentieth Century-Fox to produce the show. The ABC memo stated: "When ABC is spending its own money for deficit financing, we lose the ability to 'persuade' the utmost in production values from the producer."

In view of such boasts, the networks have found it impossible to claim immunity from charges that they are responsible for the surfeit of violence on television. That the appearance of violence is the result of deliberate efforts to capture audiences on the part of the networks was attested to by several prominent writers and producers who appeared before the House Committee on Interstate and Foreign Commerce in August 1976. David Rintels, president of the Writers Guild of America, West, said: "There is so much violence on television because the networks want it." And producer Norman Lear echoed this statement: "The simple fact is that if the networks had not wished gratuitous violence on the airwaves they control, it would not have been there."

More than ten years before the Rintels and Lear statements, another congressional committee had heard a similar story. This committee was investigating the problems of juvenile delinquency. Eventually the investigation meandered into the television connection. A network executive was called to testify about a series that the committee found unusually violent. The network did not have a contractual relationship with the producer of the series, yet when the smoke had cleared away one network executive was fired and another was on his way out.

This investigation, which began in 1961, was directed by the late Senator Thomas Dodd of Connecticut. Dodd had a long though not entirely distinguished career; he left office in disgrace after the disclosure of unethical financial campaign practices. Before leaving, Dodd had been one of the congressional masters of the art of headline hunting. As the doughty champion of the comfortable, conforming, righteous folks who were the foundation of his constituency, he reveled in the role of curmudgeon, God's angry man exposing and facing down the forces of evil.

The hearings of the juvenile delinquency subcommittee proved disappointing to headline hunters. Apparently the subject had become dated. Then someone on the committee came up with the bright idea of investigating television as the cause of juvenile delinquency. The theory was that juveniles watch violent acts being performed on TV, imitate them, and thus become delinquents.

Reporters paid attention. The committee darkened their chambers and watched action-adventure shows. The real problems of juvenile delinquency (poverty, unemployment, social inequity) were all but forgotten, except in the assumption that what appeared on the television screen was connected to what happened on the street.

During the height of the investigation the committee subpoenaed Ivan Tors, the producer of a half-hour series called "Man and the Challenge." Previous to "Man and the Challenge," which had been well received by critics, Tors had been the producer, until he was fired, so he believed, at the network's behest, of a show called "Malibu Run," which trafficked heavily in violence. Tors believed he was fired because he had neglected to heat up the episodes. Tors talked briefly about the "Malibu Run" incident, and then volunteered the more interesting story of the program he was currently working on. He explained that "Man and the Challenge," which ran from 8:30 to 9:00 on NBC, was an adventure show in which the hero, a kind of scientist, measured the limits of human physical ability and endurance under various perilous conditions. The hero wrestled with steers in rodeos, went to Mexico to fight bulls, and drove fast cars under hazardous conditions. This was one of the last prime-time series to be sold directly to an advertiser, depriving the network of an immediate contractual link to the producer. But the advertiser had to get his desired time slot from NBC, and the network let it be known that the series would not run if it ignored the pieties of the genre.

The advertising-agency executive assigned to this account told Tors that NBC had liked the pilot but didn't consider it strong enough to beat the Saturday-night competition. The ad man made it clear that the series lacked "sav," shorthand for "sex and violence." Robert Kintner, president of NBC, was responsible for the shorthand. Overnight the "sav" order became known as the Kintner edict.

Excited by these revelations, the Dodd committee subpoenaed the files of the production company, United Artists. After the committee counsel had read into the record a number of internal memos attesting to further discussion of the Kintner edict between NBC executives and United Artists' representatives, Dodd read a memo from United Artists' creative head, one Richard Dorso, addressed to John L. Sinn, president of the company. The document casts light on some of the problems of the producer, but that is not why the wily senator read it.

Dorso wrote that violence, given the hero's athletic tendencies, was not a problem. Sex was more complicated. "Sex is a two way street," he noted. The hero, Barton, "is the bright colored fly on the hook that will attract women. And physically he comes equipped for it. We should undress Barton as much as possible in every episode. He has a fine physique and those rippling muscles should be displayed at every opportunity. . . . He has no time for women, they fight for it, some succeed in getting it, but mostly he's off again in pursuit of his next brush with death. . . . That's for women."

As for men, Dorso continued, "It's that old standby, girls." NBC wanted a sexy young female who would be the hero's inamorata in every episode. Dorso opposed this concept because she would have to be the scientist's secretary or assistant, not the sort of role which would create a satisfactory relationship for future stories. The memo speculated on the results.

(1) The secretary would be an anemic, adoring hero-boss one, with her staring at him with poodle eyes while she said: "You've had a long day, Sigmond, you're tired, you should rest," or (2) a relationship where Barton, stripped to the waist, turns to somebody and says: "Do you know my assistant?" At this time his "assistant" has been making a pass at him (or him at her) and the show goes out the window with a laugh line.

Dorso preferred using a different girl in each episode.

The writers should bear in mind that most of these girls will be beautiful bitches with one end in mind, the seduction of Barton. . . . Playing Nader [George Nader, the actor who was to portray Barton] tough and hard to get . . . against a violent physical action background with a seductive, beautiful girl each week, should get the result we all want. . . . It is consistent and correct with Barton's character to have him try to resist all the warm, full blown, wealthy, determined girls who want him to spend the rest of his life on their yachts living in luxury and going soft eating bon-bons. But he likes what he's doing better which will please the critics and the PTA and at the same time be sexier, be more violent, and have more conflict. (He's got his clothes off, he's trying to put them back on and she won't let him; conflict.)

Robert Kintner was a witness on the last day of the Dodd committee hearings. He denied ever ordering the inclusion of any "improper elements" of sex or violence in "Man and the Challenge." He said he merely thought the series needed "more dramatic action" and could use "more romantic interest," language which, some people in the industry felt, did not speak to the issue. Only a few months before, the committee had heard testimony from Maurice Unger, a West Coast studio production head: "Our files contain letters from networks cautioning against excessive violence. But these letters are not always consistent with phone calls saying: '... needs more sex—needs blacker antagonists so that we can kill them off in a big climax.'"

One of the advantages of producing series for syndication is that the producer is usually free of outside influence over his creative function. Companies that are now making shows for the prime-time access period are rediscovering the joys of independence. When there are 60 to 150 different buyers it is clearly impossible for the buyer to usurp the producer's function; no single buyer is that important to the supplier.

In the mid 1950s, when I was associated with one of the many companies that specialized in first-run syndication, I ran into an exception to this independence; it was my only experience with "advertiser influence." In those days it was not uncommon for a syndicator to sell to a large regional advertiser, or to a national advertiser who wanted to spot his message in twenty or thirty specific cities. I went to a southern city to audition the pilot film of a series that one of the large cigarette companies wanted to sponsor. The company's advertising agency had recommended the show and it required only the formal approval of the tobacco company's president to close a rather substantial deal. The audition was held in the corporation's board room, where after a pregnant delay, the president appeared, surrounded by junior executives. The lights went down, the pilot unfolded. It wasn't a bad picture; as I remember it was a pretty good private-eye half-hour adventure. But I saw only its weak spots. At length the "heavy" was clamped in irons, the hero took flippant leave of the temporary sex interest, hinting at even more exciting adventure to come—and the lights went on.

There was a long pause. At length the president spoke:

"It's good. I like it. There is just one thing wrong."

"What's that?" I asked.

"Everybody in the picture is smoking short cigarettes." (The tobacco company had recently switched to the king-sized variety.) We made the deal. The president did not insist, but in the ensuing episodes, the characters smoked long cigarettes.

6

The Networks and the News

"There is a news monopoly. This situation is bad enough in the industrial and other key resource areas, but it is even more dangerous when it overrides the intentions of the First Amendment, one of the structural bases on which the constitutional system of efficient government was based."
—Jann S. Wenner, editor of *Rolling Stone*

The networks have never permitted outside production of television news. Even during the days when the advertisers owned and independent companies produced the entertainment programs, news was the exclusive domain of ABC, NBC, and CBS. Although today the news department is one of the most profitable branches of each of the companies, it was treated during the first decade of television as a public-service operation that depended upon the profits from entertainment shows for its continued existence. News was lumped in the same category with the occasional informational documentaries, classical music concerts, and other "high culture" presentations as the justification for the networks' swollen profits in the rest of their schedule.

During one of his appearances before congressional committees, Frank Stanton talked about the relation of "entertainment" to "public service" programs. CBS had just presented a one-hour concert by the eminent pianist Vladimir Horowitz. When Stanton was asked by committee chairman Hale Boggs to explain what appeared to be his network's gigantic profits, Stanton said that CBS could not run programs that were not lucrative without substantial profits from other categories. He added casually, using the indefinite article to stress his point, "For example, this extra return made it possible for us to bring you a Horowitz."

Chairman Boggs appeared puzzled. "Mr. Stanton," he asked, "what is a 'horowitz'?"

Unfortunately, Boggs knew even less about the functioning of the network monopoly and the television system than he did about concert pianists. If he had been better acquainted with the business he was investigating, he might have asked Stanton: "How many times a week do you bring us a Horowitz?"

There has always been a sharp separation between news and entertainment at CBS. The "CBS Television Network" has had no control over CBS News. In his book *Due to Circumstances Beyond Our Control,* Fred Friendly tells of a conversation he had while he headed the news department with the fabled James Aubrey, who was then president of the television network. He quotes Aubrey as saying: "They say to me, 'Take your soiled little hands, get the ratings, and make as much money as you can'; they say to you, 'Take your lily-white hands, do your best, go the high road and bring us prestige.'" Aubrey's words, according to Friendly, "could have been spoken by any of the five other presidents who preceded or succeeded him, or by any of the presidents of the other networks."

As the networks became more prosperous, so did their news operations. By the early sixties the red ink had changed to black. It was while this transformation was taking place that the networks, through their news departments, decided to take over the entire area of documentary production. A once-thriving group of producers who specialized in making informational, news, sports, and cultural documentary films for television are now out of business or dependent upon ordinary entertainment shows for their survival.

This network policy first gained publicity in 1960 when documentary producer David L. Wolper made a one-hour film called "Race for Space." Produced in cooperation with the Department of Defense and also using film supplied by the Soviet Union, the show dealt with the history of rocketry since 1900, culminating in the rivalry between the Russians and the Americans for space conquest. Wolper sold the program to a sponsor, and together they tried to get a network time period for it. They failed. The network stated its position in a letter from Frank Stanton to Senator John Pastore of Rhode Island. Stanton said that the network must "retain full responsibility for news and public affairs programs," and that such responsibility can "best be discharged through our practice of producing such programs and requiring that news and public affairs personnel be employees of, and hence accountable to, CBS News."

Wolper complained to the FCC's network study committee: "If the networks would only open the window you would find that a lot of fresh air . . . would blow into the television scene and the public would get the advantage of the exposure to new and exciting programming."

The networks had stated a "good reason" for their position,

but was it the real reason? In 1968, historian and Far East authority Theodore White wrote and narrated a ninety-minute special documentary on China for the Xerox Corporation. Xerox was unable to get any of the networks to put the program on the air, so it was distributed in syndication to over one hundred stations. A few years later, when President Nixon announced his surprise trip to China, Xerox commissioned an update of the program. New film footage was obtained and the script was rewritten and narrated by White, the entire project being subject to his control. At about the same time, White became an employee of CBS. Mindful of the Stanton emphasis on the importance of the CBS employment relationship in these situations, I advised the advertising agency for Xerox that this time they might be able to get a time slot on CBS. I was wrong. CBS refused; they had not produced the show. Xerox had to go into syndication again, with disappointing rating results.

Jacques Cousteau, inventor of the self-contained underwater-breathing apparatus (scuba) and world-famous underwater researcher, produced, directed, and "acted" in thirty-six undersea explorations, all of which appeared as specials on the ABC network over a nine-year period. The original contract for broadcast was made with ABC, which conceded that in so esoteric an enterprise Cousteau would not be subject to ABC's control except as far as general standards and practices were concerned. All went well for five years. Then for unexplained but apparently organizational reasons, the remaining Cousteau programs were placed under the jurisdiction of ABC News. They were, after all, documentaries. True to form, the news department demanded a clause in the new Cousteau license agreement giving it complete and final control over the program content. Cousteau refused. The idea that some landlubber would tell him how or what to produce was anathema. The ABC news heads stood fast on their "responsibility." In an effort to resolve the impasse, Cousteau offered to defer to the network completely if he should ever in any of his adventures touch on a subject of a political nature, but ABC was adamant. The shows went on anyway, without a signed contract.

The networks' rigid enforcement of the rule against independently produced news documentaries proved to be embarrassing to them in 1977. Early that year, David Frost, the British journalist and broadcast personality, had contracted with Richard Nixon for a series of television interviews. It was to be the former President's first public appearance since he was forced to resign his office, and it promised not only to give him an opportunity to tell his side of the story of the events that led to his downfall, but to reveal "inside information" not hitherto made public.

David Frost tried to sell the Nixon interviews to all three networks, but holding to their rule they turned him down. Later on, ABC explained further that it considered it wrong to pay a public figure for a news interview. Neither of the other two networks had that excuse; CBS had recently paid former Nixon assistant H. R. Haldeman for an interview with Mike Wallace, whereas NBC candidly admitted it had offered a fee to Nixon (reported in the *New York Times* as $400,000) only to be outbid by Frost.

Frost was forced to distribute the five interview programs by syndication. He sold some commercial announcements to national advertisers and allowed the stations to sell the rest locally. The first interview was telecast on May 4, 1977, over 155 stations, and, according to Nielsen, it was probably the most popular news interview in television history. The network-owned-and-operated stations would not accept the program, of course, so in New York, Los Angeles, and Chicago it ran on independent stations. But because of the news value of the event, the nation was treated on May 4 and May 5, 1977, to the spectacle of all three network newscasts devoting at least half their time to speculating about what would be said on the first interview program, and later to a review and editorial commentary of what had been said. In order to preserve the rerun value of the broadcasts for future use Frost refused to allow the networks to carry visual excerpts of the program, but ABC circumvented this restriction by videotaping a family watching the Nixon interview on their television set. ABC devoted time to Barbara Walters's confrontation with Frost (the interviewer being interviewed) about human-interest details of the taping session ("Did Nixon cry?" "There's a thin line between a glisten and a tear.")

One of the ironies of this incident is the fact that the first interview went on the air at 8:30 P.M. Its contents had been carefully embargoed, but enough had been let out so that the leaks became the lead story on all three television network newscasts earlier that same evening. The superficial "headline" techniques of these newscasts became "teasers" for watching the entire interview soon to come on a rival station—or if on the same station, only because some other program preferred by the network had been preempted.

The real problem posed by network control over the broadcasting of news, and anything that can be corralled into that category, is not avarice. It is the power, the potential to influence people's minds and actions, that is most troublesome. It is a disturbing fact that today most Americans do not read newspapers. Sixty percent of all Americans depend solely on television for their news.

Early in this century it was popular to decry the power entrusted to William Randolph Hearst because he owned newspapers in ten or a dozen of our largest cities. Although there were competing papers in all those cities, it was nevertheless a cause for alarm that an organization headed by one man should be able to deliver "news" to so many people. In some circles Hearst was blamed for the Spanish-American War. ("Remember the Maine" was Hearst's jingoistic slogan, and when a photographer whom he sent to Cuba to take pictures of the war of rebellion cabled that there was no war to photograph, Hearst is reported to have cabled back: "You furnish the pictures; I'll furnish the war.")

Compared to the power of a network president today, Hearst's was slight. The potential for manipulation and control of public opinion that now exists in the top offices of American networks is without question beyond any preexisting private power in our history. This fact was dramatized on November 13, 1969, when Vice-President Spiro Agnew spoke, not impartially, of a "little group of men who . . . wield a free hand in selecting, presenting, and interpreting the great issues in our nation." He then asked: "Is it not fair and relevant to question [the] concentration [of power] in the hands of a tiny, enclosed fraternity of privileged men elected by no one and enjoying a monopoly sanctioned and licensed by the government?"

While premier of France, Pierre Mendès-France once observed that "to govern is to choose." Likewise, a network's decision about how much time to devote to, say, a disarmament conference, represents a choice about the significance of that piece of news. As a matter of legality, it is not censorship to devote a thirty-minute news program to Pete Rose's salary, fighting in Beirut, the murder of a fashion designer in New York, and the price of oil, all of which may be significant pieces of news, while choosing to mention only in passing that the Soviets and Americans have not been able to agree on a time schedule for limiting the production of nuclear warheads. The reporting of news in any medium is a matter of selection, although not, as some broadcasters will claim, a purely neutral matter in which the broadcaster serves as a kind of medium chosen by particular events. In television, where the limitations of time are proportionately more stringent than the limitations of space in a newspaper, the problem of selection is intensified.

Newspapers often censor themselves without permanent damage to the body politic. Theoretically, there is no limit to the number of newspapers we can have; there are no physical or mechanical impediments that keep someone from starting up a newspaper. (I say "theoretically" because of the problem of raising the large amount of capital necessary for such a venture.) But no Horatio Alger, no matter how resourceful, can create a television channel.

Even newspaper self-censorship can be extremely dangerous. I live in a small town served by only one newspaper. As a suburban community, we are covered by metropolitan radio and television services that cannot be expected to concentrate on local problems that affect less than one-half of 1 percent of their coverage area. A few years ago an extremely damaging political scandal failed to appear in the columns of the newspaper; those of us who fought the issue were frustrated by this omission in the midst of a little iron-curtained community. We met the problem by scraping together enough money to print our own mininewspaper and mailing it to every citizen in the community, which had the effect of forcing the daily paper to print the facts. But how does one "reply in kind" to a television network? The so-called Fairness Doctrine requires television stations to permit access to their channels by those who seek to reply to a controversial statement, but neither the Fairness Doctrine nor any other rule provides for a reply to silence.

Let us suppose there is an item of legitimate news damaging to the three networks which they choose to ignore in their newscasts. Since it is "local" to but one city, the stations in all other cities do not have access to it for their news reports. This means that to at least 60 percent of the United States population that event never occurred.

Such censorship by silence has already taken place. Under the current law, television stations are licensed by the FCC for a period of three years. During that time they are not threatened by any challenger who would like to take over their channel. Although, as we have noted, the commission is not in the habit of denying license renewals, the end of the three-year period always poses the danger that some outside group may persuade the commission that the licensee has not done a good job for the community and that they, the outsiders, could do better. At best it forces the station owner to run for reelection, as it were, and to pay heed to the demands of local public service once every three years. Naturally, station owners would like to lengthen this period. That is why in 1973 the trade association representing the stations, the National Association of Broadcasters, hired an experienced lobbyist and set to work to get Congress to extend the license period to five years. The networks, owning fifteen of the most important stations in the country, were in the forefront of the lobbying assault and were supported by members of the Federal Communications Commission, anxious to reduce their workload.

Although the proposal went through many legislative stages,

was debated in committee and on the floor of each house of Congress, and was the subject of a considerable amount of discussion and controversy, the television newscasts maintained a strange and stony silence. In their book *Power, Inc.,* Morton Mintz and Jerry Cohen describe what happened: "Many owners and managers comfortably insulate themselves from . . . the handling of news about one's own enterprise that concerns the outside community. Repeatedly, for example, networks and broadcasters have ignored hearings on, objections to, and the course of legislation designed to immunize them from effective challenges to their licenses to use the public's airwaves."

In other words, you had to read the newspapers to find out what was going on. If you read John O'Connor's column in the *New York Times* on June 30, 1974, you would have learned this: "If all goes according to the plan of the National Association of Broadcasters, chief lobbying arm for the broadcast industry, the script might make an interesting TV series called 'The Great American Ripoff Machine.' It would be the program that asks the question: How do you make a powerful industry almighty?"

Edward R. Murrow hosted the first "See It Now" telecast over the CBS network on November 18, 1951. In those days the broadcast was live. As both the Brooklyn Bridge and the Golden Gate Bridge appeared on the screen simultaneously Murrow said: "For the first time in the history of man we are able to look at both the Atlantic and Pacific coasts of this great country at the same time. . . . No journalistic age was ever given a weapon for truth with quite the scope of this fledgling television."

In television, news is not selected purely on the basis of importance. We are all familiar with the fact that much obviously trivial matter is crammed in simply because it is "visual." It lends itself to the use of tape so that we have something more than a reporter talking to us across a desk.

Items of news, like everything else in the medium, are picked because they appeal to the kind of audience that is so commercially attractive that it will bring maximum dollars from an advertiser. In an address to news directors in 1977, David Brinkley elucidated the difference between television news and ordinary news.

Brinkley said,

> Ours is a mature and serious news medium and it is time we had our own standards of news judgment, instead of those handed down to us from the newspapers ... And if it is news in a newspaper, is it not also news on radio and television? No, it is not, and for a basic reason we all know but tend to forget. ... In a newspaper you can skip around, read what is interesting to you, and ignore the rest. While on a news broadcast you have to take it as it comes, in order. A newspaper can print things most of its readers don't give a damn about, because those who don't give a damn about them can skip them and go on to something else. We can't. So, what does that mean? In my opinion, it means we should not put a story on the air unless we believe it's interesting to at least ten percent of the audience—preferably more, but at least ten percent. ... I do not suggest more light or frivolous news, or more laughs. What I do suggest is that the news judgments the newspapers and wire services have developed over generations may be fine for them, but not for us. We should stop using their habits and practices, and develop our own. We should not bore the audience any more than necessary.

Television possesses extraordinary powers to communicate. Not only can it reveal people and events; in the process of revealing them it exposes its own methods and motives. In *The View from Highway 1,* Michael Arlen points out that essential to this process is an exercise of priorities: "There has to be a willingness on the part of the communicator to communicate *this* particular story, to put his bets on *this* particular event, to choose to make *this* process clear." The point is that the television communicator is guided by the entertainment quotient of his audience, haunted by the Brinkley dictum that if they don't find the news sufficiently interesting or entertaining they will switch to another channel.

Fred Friendly puts it concisely: "Because television can make so much money doing its worst, it often cannot afford to do its best." Friendly resigned in anger from his post as chief of CBS News because the network had refused his request to do live morning broadcasts of the hearings of the Senate foreign relations committee on continuation of the Vietnam War, choosing instead to do reruns of a ten-year-old program, "I Love Lucy." CBS management said this was a simple business decision: "There are times when responsible business judgments have to determine how much coverage of the Vietnam War one network and its shareholders can fiscally afford." Friendly replied that the running of the "Lucy" repeats was not a matter of deciding between two broadcasts, "but a choice between interrupting the morning run of the profit machine—whose only admitted function was to purvey six one-minute commercials every half-hour, all of which had been viewed hundreds of times before—or electing to make the audience privy to an event of overriding national importance taking place in a Senate hearing room at that very moment."

In 1978, CBS again demonstrated its view of the importance of rating points. At nine o'clock of the evening of February 1,

President Carter delivered a "Fireside Chat" on the then-pending Panama Canal treaties. ABC and NBC preempted their regular programming to bring the President's message to their viewers. CBS, however, telecast a made-for-television movie entitled "See How She Runs," and ran a tape of the President's broadcast at 11:30 P.M., during the less valuable late-night time period. It ought to be noted that some CBS affiliates did not follow their parent's lead; they broadcast the President's message live and delayed "See How She Runs" until 11:30.

Not only is the news the product of careful selection by the medium's news organizations, but the personalities of the people who "front"—the anchormen, commentators, celebrities— are the result of the sort of selection process that goes into picking any entertainer. Tests are conducted, questionnaires are distributed in order to find the "right" (usually neutral) personalities who confront us each evening. Extensive promotion campaigns are then conducted, including ballyhooing stories about the salaries of Barbara Walters and other news "stars." If Walters gets a million dollars, it isn't because she is a more discerning analyst than a rival who gets less. She is worth it at the box office, the Nielsen Television Index reports. News commentators are akin to actors who are given personalities, whether friendly, funny, gruff, sour, attractive, or sardonic.

Way back in January 1961 Robert Sarnoff, then president of NBC, in an address to a group of automobile dealers likened television to the assembly-line production of motor cars, saying, "We redesign and retool constantly to reach as many customers as possible." That is why one felt an attack of déjà vu upon reading a 1976 speech by Jann S. Wenner to the University of Southern California School of Journalism, in which he said: "Any number of studies and surveys have shown that television is the single most important source of news today. We don't have a freewheeling, competitive, diverse, unrestricted free press as was contemplated by the First Amendment, but a Government regulated monopoly. We have a Big Three in New York just as we have a Big Three in Detroit. And what has happened to news is no different from what has happened to cars; we are offered products that are essentially similar, inefficient, and unresponsive to the public interest."

Wenner voiced the usual complaint against television, applying it to newscasts that "encourage the simplistic, superficial sloganeering that conceals and distorts complexities of personality, policy and philosophy." He concluded by saying that "three networks each seeking for the same audience, are not capable of providing the diversity of views and competition for ideas which fully and broadly report the subtleties of our society and those who propose to govern it."

Mark R. Levy, a lecturer in sociology at the State University of New York at Albany, conducted intereviews with 240 adults during October and November 1975 in Albany County as part of a two-year study of the audience for local and network television news programs. Levy, who had been a writer, editor, and producer with NBC News, found that two-thirds of the respondents said that newscasters' jokes "make the news easier to take," that three-fourths liked TV news because it is often "very funny," while more than half said that watching TV makes them relax and 40 percent reported that the late news helped them fall alseep. Levy's interviews showed that one-third of the viewers chose their local news program because of the entertainment program that preceded or followed it; the next most common reason was a preference for the anchorman (20 percent of the local-news audience and 40 percent of the network viewers); less than one viewer in ten said that "news quality" was the prime reason for tuning in. That last figure raises the question of whether the reason that so few people look for television news quality is that they don't want it or that they are not conditioned to find it. This is akin to the question discussed earlier, whether ratings mean that people like what they get on television, or whether they merely submit to whatever is offered at the time. Is it logical to claim that ratings prove that people would not prefer something different if it were made available to them?

Although the networks' power usually tames obstreperous politicians, there is always the possibility that television news can never be truly "free," within the meaning of our constitutional guarantees, because the power to license television stations rests with the federal government. Thus, when President Nixon unleashed Vice-President Agnew on the television medium, there was, despite all the umbrage taken at network headquarters, a visible reduction of aggressiveness in the reporting of unpleasant news.

Agnew had criticized what he called "instant analysis" by network commentators immediately upon the conclusion of a presidential broadcast. William Paley, chairman of the board of CBS, ordered the television network to cease the practice at once. Also, for reasons they never bothered to explain, all three networks refused copies of the secret Pentagon papers that had been offered to them at the same time that newspaper editors eagerly accepted them.

During the period when Woodward and Bernstein were writing some of their most important Watergate revelations, between mid-September and Election Day in 1972, NBC devoted a total of forty-one minutes and twenty-one seconds to the break-in, while ABC took forty-two minutes and twenty-six seconds. CBS did more; there was a Walter Cronkite special on the subject on October 7, 1972, in retaliation for which, as reported by David Halberstam in *The Atlantic* (February 1976), Nixon's aide Charles Colson threatened Frank Stanton with "We'll break your network."

Perhaps the most dramatic example of the television industry's sensitivity to government reaction occurred while Lyndon Johnson was President. Johnson had had a speech prepared by his assistant, Joseph Califano, in which the term *public airwaves* had appeared. President Johnson penciled in *'s* after the word *public,* so that it now read "public's airwaves." The next day Califano was besieged by all the major broadcast lobbyists, who wanted to know whether this change signified some dangerous new anti-industry policy in the executive office.

The networks boast that they brought the Vietnam War into our living rooms, but there is reason to believe that what they brought was largely a fiction. What we saw was what Michael Arlen describes as "a parade of film clips of guns firing and of smoke rising and of refugees fleeing," a collection of images that smacked of thoughtlessness. Over a period of ten long years, television failed to tell us the major story of our times, the truth behind the tragic venture into Southeast Asia and all that it might portend for our country. The fact that our involvement in Vietnam resulted in 56,000 of our own men being killed, 156,000 wounded, and cost $155 billion that might otherwise have been used to combat poverty in America and in other parts of a hungry world moved Arlen to add: "It is a matter not of providing more combat footage, or more snapshots of human misery, or even more routine documentaries on corruption in Saigon, but, rather, of acknowledging the true scope and texture of the subject, and finding the talent . . . to master it: either as a great single work . . . or as several linked, separate works, adding up to a coherent whole; or, at least, one wherein the terrible magnitude of the subject might for once be meshed with the commitment of the faceless but powerful network authorities." Arlen wonders what might have happened

> if the networks had chosen to seriously acknowledge their role as journalists, as something more than transmitters of certified events, and had given their correspondents honest reportorial missions and had then stood behind them. After all, was Lyndon Johnson's hold on the warrior spirit of the nation so secure that he would finally have compelled a network *not* to report, say, the chaotic forced uprootings of Vietnamese that so disastrously occurred from 1966 to 1969? Did the businessmen of the nation . . . have such an irrational stake in our Indochina adventure that if NBC, CBS, and ABC had said: "Look, it is different from what the politicians and Generals say, from what you think or hope; technology will not win this war; more often, too, we are destroying rather than creating," they would have ceased to sponsor network programs?

After agreeing that television news alone would not have solved the problem of Vietnam, Arlen concludes: "I think it is evasive and disingenuous to suppose that, in its unwillingness over a space of ten years to assign a true information-gathering function to its news operations in Washington and Vietnam, American network news did much beyond contribute to the unreality, and thus the dysfunction, of American life."

The potential of the network monopoly to manipulate or simply not inform the American public is tremendous. Yet, paradoxically, the networks are constrained to relative impotence by fear—fear of government action against the licenses of their owned-and-operated stations, and fear of a loss of audience with a resultant loss of revenue. As usual, it all boils down to the dollar.

In a speech to broadcast news directors, Edward R. Murrow said that television news is a combination of show business, advertising, and news. "There is no suggestion here," he said, "that networks or individual stations should operate as philanthropies. But I can find nothing in the Bill of Rights or the Communications Act which says that they must increase their net profits each year, lest the Republic collapse."

7

Censorship:
Public or Private?

"The impact of television and radio has grown at an astonishing rate, and broadcasting promises to become by far the most influential medium of communication in our society. As its power continues to grow, preservation of Free Speech will hinge largely on zealously protecting broadcasting from censorship."
—Judge David Bazelon, of the United States Court of Appeals, March 16, 1977

The networks' monopolistic power would seem to make them a natural target for legal action. As we have seen, this is not so simple from a practical point of view. Over the past 150 years Americans have controlled natural monopolies such as gas, electricity, water, and the telephone by creating administrative agencies that regulate the prices that are charged for service. Commercial television's costs are paid by advertisers, and what they pay has never been the issue. Recommendations for government regulation of television have always been attacked by the networks as efforts to control thought. The networks have contested almost every criticism of their business practices on the grounds that it violates their constitutional guarantee of freedom of speech.

The conflict between program content and the right of freedom from censorship by the government is almost as old as commercial television itself. When the time for the first license renewals rolled around at the end of 1950, the FCC announced that it had a right to "go into" the matter of "off-color jokes, plunging necklines, and crime dramas during children's viewing hours." The FCC, however, did not act upon its own sentiments. The first speech by a member of Congress on what was to prove a popular subject for congressional oratory was made in 1951 by Thomas J. Lane, a representative from eastern Massachusetts. He quoted then-Archbishop Cushing of Boston, who, like himself, deplored "lewd images," a reference, in part, to the rather modest cleavage of an actress named Faye Emerson.

By 1960, congressional investigators were concentrating on complaints that a steady diet of intensified violence was being fed to young people from the television screen, and that this was a prime cause of the current wave of juvenile delinquency. Researchers sampled network prime-time shows and counted over one hundred weekly murders plus numerous knifings, bludgeonings, and assaults, the exact number of which depended upon the viewer's definition of the terms. It was pointed out that the more ferocious and brutal of these scenes were repeated two and three times, both as "teasers" before the show and as "previews of next week." The repetition revealed why the violence was pumped into the show in the first place.

Testifying at a Senate investigation into juvenile delinquency in 1961, Dr. Wilbur Schramm said that television crime and brutality were a "trigger" for youthful offenders. "The amount of violence is just too dangerous to go on." Fifteen years later, Congressman Timothy Wirth of Colorado demanded a new FCC investigation, and called "network programs, loaded with violence, crime and sex, a national disgrace." In 1972, after three years of study, the United States surgeon general's scientific advisory committee published five volumes, concluding that "at least under some circumstances, exposure to television aggression can lead children to accept what they have seen as a partial guide for their own actions." And: "A significant position correlation has been found much more often than not [between watching TV violence and "aggressive behavior in adolescents"] and there is no negative correlational evidence." And: "More overt aggressive behavior follows exposure to violent content than to nonviolent content."

It has always seemed to me that the real evil is not that the viewer, whether child or adult, will imitate the action portrayed in a fictional drama, so much as that he is taught, day in and day out, hour by hour, that all problems are solved by violence, that every wrong can be righted and every ending made happy by a simple punch in the jaw or bullet in the belly.

Professors of communication George Gerbner and Larry Gross point out that although there may be some awareness that a particular event is fictional, we expect, and often demand, that dramatic narrative be true to life. The viewer is thus subjected to a stream of "facts," which are presented as if they were absolute statements about human nature. After watching television long enough, even relatively sophisticated viewers may begin to believe that all people are either good or bad, stupid or brilliant, shiftless or dynamic—in short, cops or robbers.

In this "realistic" television world, one-fifth of all living beings are engaged in law enforcement. One-third of the people portrayed on the television screen come either from the ranks of official or semiofficial police authority, or from the ranks of criminals, outlaws, spies, and other enemies of the law. Violence, of course, plays a major role in such a world. If it is visible, flashy, dramatic, it not only can answer all questions but it can tie up all loose ends within the hour.

In one of their studies, Gerbner and Gross sent questionnaires to groups screened on the basis of education, amount of newspaper reading they did, gender, economic status, and age. Each of these groups was divided in turn into two parts, heavy television viewers and light television viewers. In all cases and in all groups, the heavy television viewers gave answers indicating that they saw the real world as more dangerous and frightening than did the light television viewers. To such questions as "Can most people be trusted?" and "During any given week what are your chances of being involved in some type of violence—1 in 10 or 1 in 100?" and "What proportion of the population is engaged in law enforcement?" they found that college education and regular newspaper reading reduced the percentage of those who viewed the world as extremely dangerous and frightening, while heavy TV viewing boosted that percentage within both groups. Also, television appeared to condition the reaction of the generation that never knew life without it, the figures indicating that the "under 30" respondents showed higher levels of "dangerous world responses" despite the fact that they tended to be better educated than the "over 30" respondents. According to Gerbner and Gross, "we may all live in a dangerous world, but young people . . . , the less educated, women, and heavy viewers within all these groups sensed greater danger than light viewers in the same groups . . . Since most TV 'action-adventure' dramas occur in urban settings, the fear they inspire may contribute to the current flight of the middle-class from our cities. The fear may also bring increased demands for police protection, and election of law-and-order politicians."

In the summer of 1978, Florida was the scene of the murder trial of Ronney Zamora, a fifteen-year-old boy who in the course of a robbery had shot and killed an elderly female neighbor. His defense was that at the moment he pulled the trigger, he was "legally insane," that is, he did not know right from wrong, and that this insanity resulted from his addiction to watching his favorite show, "Kojak," as well as other action dramas on television. According to the testimony of his parents, Ronney had come to the United States from Cuba at the age of five unable to speak English, and he had learned the English language by watching television for approximately eight hours a day every day for the next ten years. Zamora's attorney argued that the boy had become "subliminally intoxicated" by the prolonged viewing of television programs, especially by those depicting explicit violence. He told the jury that over a ten-year period his client had seen approximately fifty thousand television murders and this constant exposure to the taking of human life by the heroes as well as the villains had given him a warped idea of human values and behavior. The lawyer concluded his summation with an attack on television as a medium.

> Television has changed when we eat and when we sleep and when we kill and when we don't kill and how to kill, and the good guys can kill, and the bad guys can kill, and it all comes on the tube again next week, same time, same station. . . . Now

they've invented a machine that in case there's a murder on one channel and you want to see a rape on another channel, you can hook up this machine and it records the channel you're not watching ... you don't miss a thing. ... It's time we did something.

That this argument was ineffective with the jurors was demonstrated not only by their quick "guilty" verdict, but by statements they made after the trial, which was itself televised, with one camera constantly in operation in the rear of the courtroom. After the verdict eight jurors were interviewed, and each said that he didn't believe that television had anything to do with the case. Some of the jurors said they liked television programs, their manner indicating a resentment of the defense attorney's attack on the medium. One male juror was especially outspoken. "I endorse any and all television," he said. "It's police shows, it's—what it is doing is bringing the everyday violence that occurs out on the street into your home and you're getting more educated."

A few weeks after the Zamora conviction Judge Robert Dossee of the California superior court ruled that a network could not be held civilly liable for negligence for showing an artificial rape on television which was later imitated by a group of teenagers. The parents of the young girl who was the victim of the crime sued the network that had broadcast the show, on the grounds that its executives were negligent in scheduling a program depicting this act during prime time, because they should have known young viewers might be tempted to imitate it. The court held that the network was protected by the First Amendment against such liability, unless the broadcast came within an exception that prohibits "deliberate incitement" to violence.

Although the ruling of Judge Dossee is a proper application of the constitutional guarantee of free speech to television—any other decision would make it impossible for a broadcaster to depict any act that might conceivably have harmful consequences for anyone—it is nevertheless also true that apologists for the industry cite the First Amendment as protection against every form of criticism they encounter. Fred Friendly has written that "the broadcaster who wraps himself in the First Amendment while clutching his franchise to his bosom is asking to have his constitution two ways." It seems apparent that the amendment was primarily intended to protect the reading public, rather than simply serve as a shield for the property rights of the speaker. "Congress shall make no law . . . abridging freedom of speech, or of the press," says the clause, and broadcasters are quick to claim that they are part of the press and that the press is named "as an institution" for specific protection. Nevertheless, it is difficult to take seriously the constitutional claims that are based on the insistence on what former FCC commissioner Nicholas Johnson called "profitable speech, not free speech." The real censorship that the viewer faces comes not from the government, but from the industry itself.

This problem was dramatized by some widely publicized events beginning in the fall of 1975, by which time congressional speeches on television violence had become especially pointed. But continued demands that the industry "do something about it" fell on deaf ears. The three networks were busy fighting for the audience with "action" shows, and the competition seemed to focus on the amount and intensity of the action rather than on the nature of the action itself.

As congressional complaints increased, Richard Wiley, then chairman of the Federal Communications Commission, became increasingly exercised. As he later testified, he did not have the inclination to become a censor, and he doubted whether the FCC as such had any authority to be one. After all, the Communications Act contains a specific prohibition against the FCC's interfering in program content. Nevertheless, Wiley called a meeting of the presidents of each of the three national networks, and in what he apparently considered circumspect language suggested that they ought to take measures. Wiley was using what insiders at the FCC call the "raised eyebrow technique." Later on, a federal judge was to reprove Wiley for "issuing threats of regulatory action" if no voluntary action was forthcoming.

In any event, three days later Arthur Taylor, president of CBS, announced that commencing the following fall, CBS would not permit the telecasting of any program involving sex or violence between 7:00 and 9:00 P.M. Obviously, with the high rating potential of shows containing elements of sex and certainly of those specializing in violence, it would be impossible for one network to follow such a policy alone, and the alacrity with which the other two networks agreed to adopt a similar plan suggests that a general agreement had been reached either at the Wiley conference or at some other time.

The advent of what then came to be known as the "family hour" raised a number of interesting questions. In the first place it actually was an "hour," because ever since the passage of the Prime-Time Access Rule the networks had not programmed anything other than news prior to 8:00 P.M. (7:00 P.M. Central Time). Secondly, because the Central zone has traditionally taken network programming simultaneously with the East, prime time in the Midwest is from 6:00 to 10:00 P.M., and the family hour ends at eight o'clock in that area. Based on the theory that children go to bed, or at least stop looking at television, at nine o'clock in New York, Los Angeles, Philadelphia, and San Francisco, there is now an assumption that they go to bed and stop watching television in such cities as Chicago, Milwaukee, Memphis, Omaha, Minneapolis, Kansas City, St. Louis, and New Orleans at 8:00 P.M.—no doubt one of those bits of demographic research that networks hold so dear.

In the third place, nobody bothered to define what kind of programming or what elements of programming were prohibited under the rule. It soon became clear that sex was not the main issue. With increased sexual permissiveness in theatrical motion pictures and popular magazines, it appeared that nothing that television dared do during any part of prime time would be of serious concern. Violence, however, is an entirely different story, but just what degree of violence was to be permitted has never been decided and is the cause of occasional worry and internetwork backbiting.

Finally, although the problem apparently hadn't occurred to the networks when the original agreement was made, the family-hour idea affected a broad period of time that is not included in its definition, specifically the nonnetwork "station" time during the late-afternoon and early-fringe hours. Although the rule specifies only the first two hours of prime time, it is obvious that if a show is not fit to be seen by children between 8:00 and 9:00 P.M., it isn't fit to be run by stations between 4:30 and 6:00 P.M., when the children have come home from school.

As we have noted, afternoon and fringe time has been a fertile field for the reruns of off-network programming, including the violent action-adventure dramas that still grace the networks after 9:00 P.M. The threat to future profits from the reruns of the plethora of such successful crime shows as "Kojak," "Mannix," "Hawaii Five-O," "The Rookies," "Baretta," and

"Starsky and Hutch" was real and they suffered an overnight loss running into millions of dollars.

A *TV Guide* poll conducted between October 10 and 12, 1975, by the Opinion Research Corporation found that 82 percent of adult Americans favored the family hour. But most people in the industry felt that the family hour was a public-relations gimmick. The New York bureau chief of *TV Guide* said that "while Chairman Wiley called the concept a 'landmark' and Senator Pastore said it was a 'wonderful idea,' hardly anybody, privately, considered it anything but a gentleman's agreement between Congress, the FCC, the networks, and the NAB to take the heat off all of them." Most newspaper television critics viewed the family hour as an invitation to greater and bloodier violence from 9:00 to 11:00 P.M. *Newsweek* reported that the networks simply shifted their schedules, moving violent shows from the earlier to the later time periods; *Newsweek* described the 9:00 to 11:00 P.M. segment as "a cops and robbers ghetto" containing "no less than eighteen crime shows."

Hollywood writers and directors were outraged by the family hour. They and their unions were joined by some producers who, feeling that the value of their property had been threatened, brought a lawsuit against the networks, the National Association of Broadcasters, and the FCC to bring an end to it. (The National Association of Broadcasters was named in the suit because it had arranged to have its code-review board monitor the compliance with the rule, thereby in effect giving it censorship powers.) Action shows had been relegated to the post—9:00 P.M. period, but the programs that remained on the schedule between 8:00 and 9:00, largely situation comedies, were subject to more network interference in content and theme than was typical. Writers and directors complained that certain adult topics had been prohibited, which in turn harmed the chances of success on the part of their product. Norman Lear, producer of "All in the Family," had refused to agree to network demands for what he considered substantive changes, so his show was moved from eight to nine o'clock. He assumed that this meant it would, by definition, lose its attraction as an off-network rerun in the afternoon period in the years to come.

It was a peculiar lawsuit, based on the allegation that the FCC, through its chairman, had interfered in program content and in effect made itself a government censor. It was assumed that proof of this allegation would somehow result in abolition of the rule, even though the networks had agreed to put the rule into effect and would undoubtedly keep it alive with or without government censorship.

Federal District Judge Warren J. Ferguson announced his decision on November 3, 1976. He found that Chairman Wiley, acting with the consent of the other members of the FCC, had threatened the networks with governmental action if they did not agree to curb sex and violence in their shows, and that this illegal action was an "indispensable cause" of the creation of the family hour. He also held that the National Association of Broadcasters could not set itself up nor be empowered by others to act as a television censor. But even with those findings the decision had no practical applicability. The judge could not order the networks or stations to run or not run any programs. The broadcasters have a right to exercise self-regulation, a remedy that the judge, as a matter of fact, endorsed as one answer to too much sex and violence in television. But self-regulation is often a euphemism for censorship, in this case, censorship by an agreement among the three networks.

In 1964, Associate Justice Byron R. White of the Supreme Court, referring to the protections of the First Amendment, said that "it is the right of the viewers and listeners, not the right of the broadcasters, which is paramount." Justice White pointed out that although "broadcasting is clearly a medium affected by a First Amendment interest," it is also a medium where there are more people who want to broadcast than there are channels, and thus it is foolish to claim that each one of them has a constitutional right to broadcast which is "comparable to the right of every individual to speak, write or publish."

Even though Chairman Wiley exceeded his authority in "suggesting" the institution of family hour, the FCC is not without power to enforce the requirements of such an hour as a condition for the licensing of television stations. The unpalatable and illegal aspect of censorship is what lawyers call prior restraint. The prohibition against censorship says, in effect, that you cannot prevent somebody from saying something before he says it, but it does not say that you cannot punish him afterward for having said it. The FCC has had the right to consider program content in the granting or withholding or renewing of broadcasting licenses ever since the formation of the early Radio Commission in 1927. In the commission's first case, in 1930, it denied the renewal of radio-station broadcasting rights to a Dr. Brinkley, who used the airwaves to promote the use of goat glands as a way of guaranteeing sexual potency. In that case the United States court of appeals in the District of Columbia announced that the business of broadcasting is "impressed with a public interest" and because the number of available broadcasting frequencies is limited, "the Commission is necessarily called upon to consider the character and quality of the service to be rendered." And in another case two years later, the same court added, "This is neither censorship nor previous restraint." Nor was it apparently "censorship" for the FCC to hold in 1941 that no radio stations could editorialize. In 1949 the FCC reversed that ruling and encouraged editorializing, but set up as a corollary what is called the Fairness Doctrine, which requires a station "to afford reasonable opportunity for the discussion of conflicting views on issues of public importance." (This is not to be confused with the "Equal Time" rule that makes it mandatory for a broadcaster to give the opportunity for equal time on his air to all candidates for the same elective public office. It was the Fairness Doctrine that dictated, for example, that broadcasters had to make time available for messages presenting antismoking views, because stations were then running cigarette commercials. There is an important body of opinion that opposes the Fairness Doctrine on the grounds that it has a chilling effect on the presentation by stations of any controversial views, and is itself an unconstitutional restriction on a broadcaster's right of free speech.)

Government censorship, for all of its evils, can at least be subjected to popular restraint. If what the censors are doing is bad enough to arouse public resentment, the voters can refuse to reelect the office-holders who are responsible. But to private or industry self-censorship there is no appeal, not even in theory. This distinction was brought to public attention by certain events occurring at the beginning of the 1977–78 broadcast season. Reacting to the same stimuli that had brought about the family hour, a number of advertisers issued public statements saying they were opposed to the glorification of extremely violent action as a means of getting high ratings. Simultaneously the networks disclosed their new programs for the coming season, which revealed a uniform turn toward shows preoccupied with sex—or at least with what passes for sex on television. One such program was an ABC series called "Soap," which some of the network executives predicted would certainly achieve high ratings because of a promised profusion of sexual high-jinks the like of which had never before been seen on the tube. An editorial in the *New York Times* described the series as one that "concerns the sexual predilections of members of two families, featuring a philandering husband and an impotent one, a transvestite son and a promiscuous daughter who was having an affair with a tennis pro who was having an affair with her promiscuous mother." The ABC announcement of "Soap" galvanized a wide array of church groups into counteraction. The United States Catholic Conference, the Christian Life Commission of the Southern Baptist Convention, the National Council of Churches, the United Church of Christ, the United Methodist Church, and the National Council of Catholic Bishops called for and supported protests, not only of the individual ABC stations that would carry the show, but of those business concerns that had reportedly bought advertising on the show. Within a few days a number of companies announced that they had canceled orders for commercial spots in "Soap" because of the threat of boycott of the advertised products.

Once again the cry of "censorship" was heard, this time from executives of ABC, numerous advertising agencies, and the American Civil Liberties Union. This was censorship, they said, not by government or by industry, but by "private, irresponsible groups" who were preventing other Americans from seeing what they might want to see. The action of the religious groups was likened to that of "McCarthyite red-baiters" of the early 1950s, whose threats of boycott caused sponsors to blacklist radio and television actors, writers, and directors who were suspected of left-wing sympathies.

The opposition to the boycott threat was based on two unarticulated assumptions. One was that a show cannot go on the air without advertisers; the other was that the *existing* method of program selection is by other than "private, irresponsible groups." Thus, Frederick Pierce, president of ABC Television, said it is "a very unhealthy situation when special-interest groups . . . determine what is right and what isn't for the viewing public." What he did *not* say was that he and others in his position have been making that decision by themselves and they want to continue to do so—and that they are a private "special interest group," though their interest is based on an economic rather than a moral standard.

There is little doubt that voluntary action by citizens is preferable to government censorship, and is, indeed, an antidote for it. It also seems that such action ordinarily should be confined to individual protest, and that an attempt to prevent the communication of ideas or the right to receive them, no matter how unsavory they are, should be avoided. In other words, if we don't like pornographic movies or magazines, we avoid them; we don't try to prevent others from viewing or reading them. The difficulty is that such a philosophy works only in a free market, like that of movies and the print media. The television set is in our home; when we turn it on, we watch what we are given to watch: programming that the networks believe will bring them the highest possible profit. The church groups can argue that the "pressure" that they were accused of bringing to bear was at least democratic pressure, as opposed to the self-serving financial pressure continually exerted by their adversaries.

8

The Networks' Invasion of Neighboring Domains

"The competitive advantage that defendants [networks] obtain in these re-lated areas is not a result of their skill, foresight or industry. It flows solely from each defendant's bargaining leverage obtained through its combination of governmentally acquired licenses. The restraints effected are neither ancil-lary to such licenses nor necessary for their enjoyment."
—From a memorandum filed with the United States District Court for the Central District of California by Department of Justice attorneys in *United States of America v. CBS, Inc.,* and *United States of America v. American Broadcasting Companies, Inc.,* 1978

One of the evils of unbridled monopoly power is that it en-ables the monopolist to bludgeon his way into areas related to (but not necessary to) the pursuit of his major business. It al-lows him to use his leverage to compete unfairly and drive out of business legitimate practitioners in peripheral areas. Net-work history is replete with examples of this type of gouging.

The foremost domain of the networks is the broadcast busi-ness. Networks could be networks even if they did not own any television stations. As far back as the days of radio, the networks exercised their leverage to obtain the ownership and operation of all of the affiliated stations in the nation's largest markets. Today owned-and-operated television stations account for over $100 million in annual income to the networks, and their combined worth is well over $1 billion.

When Senator Bricker of Ohio alleged in a speech in the Senate in 1956 that one network-owned television station had shown a profit of 1,834 percent on investment, and another 1,645 percent, CBS president Stanton rushed to the defense of his company. It was ridiculous to insinuate that the ownership of stations contributes to a monopoly environment, he said, because "CBS owns only 1 percent of the television stations in the United States." Inasmuch as there were then 503 stations on the air, Stanton was arithmetically correct. What he failed to say was that at that time, CBS's five stations reached not 1 percent but 25 *percent* of American television homes, and that given the fact that they had sole rights in their markets to the programming of 33.3 percent of the U. S. networks, the use of the horrid word *monopoly* in connection with them had justification.

There is, of course, no technological reason for networks to own stations. Nor is there, as there once was, an economic reason. When networks were only clearinghouses and time-sales agents for their affiliates, they depended on their owned-and-operated stations for the bulk of their profit. Indeed, their broadcast activities were the economic foundation of their existence as private entrepreneurial businesses. Otherwise they might have developed as cooperatives like the Mutual Network in radio. But since ABC, NBC, and CBS became the owners of programs and purveyors of announcements, and since they assumed the role of suppliers to the affiliates, their income from the networking business has far surpassed even the massive sums gained each year by the owned-and-operated stations. Broadcasting is truly a supplementary business to networking.

Another area invaded by the network was that of the talent agency. The agent, or "ten percenter," as he is known, because of the commission he takes from the artist's earnings, is a traditional figure in show-business circles. As the entertainment industry grew more complex with the advent of radio, so did the agencies grow, some to the size of the giant William Morris Agency with hundreds of employees and offices throughout the world. As far back as radio, it occurred to CBS and NBC that their huge power to hire and fire, to make and break actors and writers and directors, afforded them tremendous leverage in persuading these people to join their own newly formed artists' agencies. Overnight these two networks became threatening competitors to the existing companies. Any agent could promise to try to get his performer-client on a network radio show, but only a network could guarantee it. Eventually the Department of Justice made antitrust gestures toward the networks, and at about the time television came on the scene, the networks agreed to get out of this business. It had been a minor venture for them, but it demonstrated the force of their leverage.

The networks then went into the "station representative" business. All commercial television stations, network affiliates as well as independents, sell nonnetwork or "local" time to national advertisers. This is called spot advertising, meaning that the announcements are "spotted" locally rather than covering the entire country by network. The affiliated stations sell this advertising in programs that are run during station time—for example, during the late afternoons before the networks begin their nightly monopoly. They also sell time for spot announcements made during station breaks, on the hour and half-hour, commonly known as "adjacencies" (being adjacent to network programming), and they sell commercial announcements in local news and sports shows. The major advertising agencies are centered in New York City, and it is important for stations to have a representative in New York who can readily do business with these houses. Thus the occupation of station representative grew, with a single representative selling time on television stations in many cities of the country, though he handled only one outlet in the same city because of obvious conflict of interest. Since each of the three networks had four owned-and-operated television stations outside the city of New York, it was only natural for them to represent themselves insofar as those four were concerned. Once this machinery was set up, it occurred to them that there was no reason why they couldn't represent other stations, especially their own affiliates. And it would certainly take a strong and courageous affiliate to deny the parent network when it approached him for the station-representative business. The result was that overnight the station-representative firms operated by the three networks became dominant in the industry. The trade association of the dispossessed firms, the Station Representatives' Association, approached both the Department of Justice and the FCC, alleging that the networks had violated the antitrust laws by squeezing them out of their established business. After due consideration, the FCC agreed. The commission said that it recognized that the spot organizations could exert pressures on affiliates "because of the control exercised by their current organizations over affiliation and network rates." It added that the network spot-sales organizations "are in a position to extend the influence of their networks over the affiliated stations" and the networks "could use their control over network affiliations to influence the stations' choice of a spot representative. . . . This influence could be exerted directly . . . it could also be indirect and involve no overt pressure by the network. Thus, stations may have an incentive to improve their chances of acquiring or retaining a network affiliation or of securing other benefits from the network by requesting representation by network spot sales organizations."

Because the networks had "made use of a potent competitive advantage over independent national spot representatives in soliciting . . . stations affiliated with their respective networks" the commission prohibited the networks' representation of any but their owned-and-operated stations. Therefore, by 1960 this particular instance of monopolization was over. But there was more to come.

The networks had muscled their way into the station-representative business by way of their monopoly power over their affiliated stations. Far more lucrative results were obtained by exercising their monopoly power over the program producers. Their exactions fall into three categories, none of which is part of or necessary to the operation of a network. They are syndication rights, merchandising rights, and a percentage of net profits from nonnetwork uses. All three had become so pervasive that the FCC, prodded by the Department of Justice, prohibited their continuance as part of the Prime-Time Access Rule. Unfortunately, the effects of all three practices are still being felt, and will continue to be for many years.

Let us first consider network entry into the syndication business, the distribution of filmed and taped television properties to both foreign countries and U. S. television stations as reruns. The distributor has a large overhead; he has offices or representatives all over the world, and salesmen in many parts of the country. He must pay those salesmen either a substantial commission or a high salary plus travel and living expenses. The business is highly specialized and the salesman is more than just a salesman; he actually becomes a station programmer. In order to convince a buyer of the desirability of a particular show, he must understand the competitive rating situation in the city and what kind of fare would best "counter-program" his customer's rivals. Because of these problems, distribution fees run relatively high, reaching 35 or 40 percent of the total amount received from all sales of the shows in the United States, and 40 to 50 percent of everything paid outside the country.

The networks found an easy way to get into this business. They simply insisted to the producers from whom they purchased programming that the distribution rights be granted to them. This included not only the right to sell immediately in foreign countries, but the right to license the reruns in the United States in the event of the show's success. The networks ran into resistance. Most of the programs came from producers who were also in the distribution business, particularly the so-called major motion-picture companies. Thus, Universal-MCA, Paramount, Columbia, Metro-Goldwyn-Mayer, Warner Brothers, Twentieth Century-Fox, and United Artists all boasted large and successful distribution companies. As we have seen, they rely to a large extent upon the success of these distribution companies to justify the losing business of producing for network television. Nevertheless, even to these companies, and certainly to the large number of smaller and weaker independent producers, the networks fell into the habit of insisting that if they were to buy a show, the distribution rights would be theirs. Sometimes when the network dealt with a major producer for more than one series, there would be a compromise:

the network would allow the producer to distribute every other series, keeping the alternates for itself.

The networks had an easier time with those individual producers who did not operate their own distribution companies. The right to retain distribution was still extremely valuable to that independent producer because he could literally sell it to one of the major distributing companies, which would give him a cash payment or a substantial guarantee in return for getting the rights. Thus, when Norman Lear made his deal with CBS for "All in the Family," he had no choice but to give CBS the distribution rights if he wanted to get his show on the air. Some years later, after the series became a roaring success, Lear sued CBS (and Viacom, its spin-off successor in the distribution business) to get his rights back. He lost the case; the court felt he had gone along with CBS from the beginning and it wasn't until the show became a hit that he decided that he had been coerced. This may have been true, but it still leaves the essential problem unsolved.

Over a period of two decades the film-syndication subsidiaries of the three networks became the most powerful and successful companies in the business. Galling though it was for a major motion-picture company like United Artists or even an independent like Metromedia Producers to relinquish distribution to their greatest rivals, they had no choice but to comply in order to get on network air. We have already quoted the producers' adage to the effect that you have to get up to bat in order to make a hit. The network controls the "at bats," and the producer must accept many an indignity in order to get his turn at the plate.

The FCC's purpose in promulgating the Prime-Time Access Rule in 1971 was to protect and encourage independent pro-

duction as an alternative source of program supply. In addition
to prohibiting the networks from programming a half-hour of
prime time each night, the rule contained two other provisions.
One prohibited a network from obtaining a percentage of
profit or ownership in an independently produced program, a
pervasive abuse that we shall discuss later in this chapter. The
other provision forbade networks to continue to operate a syndication business; it gave the networks one year in which to
divest themselves of their syndication subsidiaries. Thus by
mid-1972, ABC had spun off its syndication subsidiary to
Worldivision, a company made up of its former employees,
while NBC's went to a company called NTA and CBS's to the
newly formed organization of CBS stockholders known as
Viacom. So extensive were the network distribution rights, especially on the part of ABC and CBS, that all three successor
companies have remained important in the business, with
Viacom the largest and most successful.

A related area of activity that the networks wormed their
way into is the business called character merchandising. This is
the practice of licensing the rights to make T-shirts and other
articles of clothing related to the chief character or characters
in a successful television series; it includes also the manufac-
ture of toys and games, the publication of paperback books
based on the stories that could be created out of the series, and
coloring books, comic books, and even phonograph records
and sheet music of the theme song. Obviously, this pursuit is
not a necessary adjunct of the network business. Though some
of the producers have their own merchandising subsidiaries,
and numerous independent merchandisers do quite well in this
area, the networks again became the most formidable opera-

tors as a result of the use of their leverage. In 1972 this business, being generally related to distribution, was spun off with the syndication operation.

The other provision of the Prime-Time Access Rule was the prohibition of the exaction by networks of a percentage of net profits accruing to a producer from nonnetwork uses of a series, such as foreign sales, domestic syndication after the completion of network showings, merchandising, spin-offs into new series using characters from the old one—anything that might develop from a successful TV series. This practice had been so pervasive that in many producer–network negotiations the only discussion of it would be how high the percentage should be. Producers got to the point where they were happy if they could keep for themselves a share as large as that demanded and obtained by the network. The common contract method was to list percentages payable to a star actor, a director, and perhaps the author of the original book on which the series was based, and to divide the remainder equally between the network and the producer.

By the 1960s there was hardly a prime-time show on the air that was exempt from this network tribute. An FCC report in 1970 set the figure at 98 percent. So widespread was the practice and so submissive were the producers that one network executive told an investigating committee that the producers were asking the network to please take a share of the profits. The reason for such philanthropy was known as far back as twenty years ago when the report of the Senate Committee on Interstate and Foreign Commerce noted that "the networks occupy such a key position, by virtue of their control over the best time in the key markets, that they have the power either to exclude independently produced programs from their schedules . . . or to give such programs access to network time only in return for the granting of an interest in the independent programs."

The excuse most often advanced by the networks for taking a profit share from later nonnetwork uses of a program was that the network was taking the risk of expending monies to develop a pilot which might never get on the air. There is little merit in this argument. In the first place, most production companies were well able to fully finance their pilots (the networks seldom paid the complete costs anyway), and in recent years, with most pilots being created as television movies (or in the case of situation comedies, as part of "comedy specials"), development losses were minimized. Furthermore, the demand for advertising time is so large and the supply so small that the networks have seldom been worried about selling a program (or spot announcements in a program) that they put on the air. In the entire history of American network television, there has never been an entertainment series that ran as a prime-time "sustainer"—that is, without advertising.

But there were many cases where a network took no financial risk whatsover, yet extracted the profit participation from the producer. I have been connected with such cases, involving all three networks. The first I can remember goes back to the days when sales were made directly to advertisers. The company with which I was associated produced at its own expense the pilot film of a series, "Tombstone Territory," which remained on the air for three years. We sold the show for a firm fifty-two weeks to the Bristol-Myers Company through its advertising agency, Young & Rubicam. Bristol-Myers had a "franchise" of a half-hour of weekly prime time on one of the networks. The program was purchased, according to customary practice, subject to approval by the network. We were unhappy but not surprised when the network said it did not approve the program; it didn't like its content. A meeting was arranged between the president of the production company and the director of programming of the network, after which it was announced that the network had changed its mind; it now approved the series—and would receive 50 percent of all net profits from nonnetwork uses after the original run. Since the pilot had been made and the series presold, the network was taking no risk.

A few years later, the same company produced, also at its own expense, the pilot of a series called "Mona McClusky." By this time it was understood that the written contract would have to be made with the network even if the producing firm succeeded in interesting an advertiser. Our company obtained the promise of full sponsorship from the Liggett & Myers Tobacco Company (this was at a time when cigarettes were still advertised over the air), but the buyer informed us that we would have to deal directly with the network, with whom it had an arrangement for the allocation of a prime-time half-hour. Liggett & Myers told us that they would let the network know that they wanted this show and would sponsor it. We then opened negotiations with the network, which insisted upon and got a percentage of our "future-uses" profit as part of the deal—even though the pilot had been made and the series presold, so the network was taking no risk.

In recent years, producers have sold television series only to networks, who in turn have sold commercial announcements in those series to advertisers. There is an occasional exception, however, where an advertiser wants to sponsor (or cosponsor with other advertisers) the entire showing of a single program called a "special," usually a 60- or 90-minute variety extravaganza or documentary feature. In this limited area the old system still prevails. The producer deals first with the advertiser and then goes through the sales process a second time with a network that might be willing to make an appropriate time period available to the advertiser. Here again the network insists that the producer sign an agreement directly with it. In each case the network knows that there is no risk, and yet, in numerous cases before the practice was stopped, the network demanded and obtained a share in the profits that the producer might get from uses beyond that original network run. It is true that for the most part the nonnetwork uses were restricted to foreign sales because the high residual payments and the heavy selling costs make domestic syndication of single-shot specials unusual (it costs just as much to sell one special as it does to sell a series of 150 episodes, with a dramatically lower return), but there are exceptions. One was a one-hour documentary special called "Time of Man." It was produced by another company with which I was associated, in conjunction with the American Museum of Natural History, and bought by the network only after we had obtained assurance of sponsorship. About the time the network had concluded its two permitted prime-time runs of this show, our company was ready to syndicate twenty-four "National Geographic" hours. Because of the similarity of subject matter, we found that many stations would add "Time of Man" to their "Geographic" purchase, and we were able to make a large number of syndication sales. The result was substantial profit checks sent to the network every three months, the share being equal to that of the producer.

There were some network executives who believed that the

business of participating in the profits of future uses of a series was related to the cost of production. But in the bargaining over what the network would pay the producer for his finished work, talk of profit sharing played no part. Both parties were aware that the chances of a series' being successful enough to pay off on profit participation were remote, the odds being around ten to one against such a happy resolution. It would be folly for a network to depend upon the eventual receipt of a profit share to make up any part of the cost of a show.

The absence of any connection between program pricing and the granting of a profit participation has been confirmed since the FCC prohibition of a network's participation in profits from future uses. The sums paid by networks for series have increased, more or less in keeping with inflation—they certainly did not go down when the practice was stopped.

Since 1972, who has been compensating the networks for their magnified "risks"? As costs have increased, so have whatever risks there are—yet the networks have been making more money than at any other time in their history.

Looking back, it becomes clear that all of the justifications were spurious. One is tempted to describe the practice as extortion, but that would imply an evil intention on the part of the network officers, which I do not believe was consciously there. I suspect they rationalized their future-use participation because they realized that it was the network and only the network that could make it possible for the producer to earn any money at all. They could say with some truth that if they did not take the show there never would be any foreign sales or postnetwork runs from which lavish profits might flow. There cannot be a *post*network run unless there is first a *network* run.

In other words, they could say that they are entitled to a share of the profits that eventuate because they put the show on *their* air.

The only trouble with that argument is that it is not their air. It belongs to the people.

9

What Can Be Done Within the System

"Those who say they give the public what it wants begin by underestimating public taste and end by debauching it."

—T. S. Eliot

To condemn all television programming is stupid. But to fail to see that the bulk of it is shoddy is equally obtuse. And the effective disenfranchisement of people who don't happen to fall within the desired demographic range fancied at the moment invites correction.

What should be done about it?

One answer is to give up on commercial television and look to alternative sources such as pay TV and public TV, the subject of the next chapter. Here, however, we will consider changes that can be made within the framework of our present commercial structure.

The most desirable change is to arrange for a system that would allow for more networks and more stations, thus ending the monopoly and creating more diverse programming.

Before Channel 13 in New York became a public television

station, it was privately operated by a group of local people. The station management conceived the idea of producing a classical drama every week. The classics were used rather than more contemporary plays because they were in the public domain; that is, because of copyright expiration there were no royalties or fees due to writers or their heirs. The programs were usually two hours long and ran twice a day six days a week, three times on Sundays. The production was entirely local, and a special deal was made with the actors' union allowing a low rerun fee for the fifteen weekly performances. Even though the plays were directed at a relatively small audience, and even with a low rating per showing, the aggregate of the telecasts made it commercially viable for advertisers. All fifteen performance ratings were put together to obtain an acceptable dollars-per-thousand cost for a commercial.

It was an example of how with enough stations one can, even under our commercial system, appeal to diverse tastes. It is comparable to what happens with respect to radio in our larger cities, where response to the large number of stations confirms the existence of a heterogeneous audience.

One sure way to get enough television channels, all with relatively equal technical potential, would be to abolish VHF transmission and have all television in the UHF band—in other words, correct the mistake that was made when stations were first licensed some thirty years ago. There could be any number of networks, depending only upon the demands of the marketplace, and there could be as much diversity of programming as the traffic would bear. The need for government regulation would be minimized, for we would have the advantage of truly free competition. At first there might even be more stations on the air than the economy could support, but so what?

Why in the case of this one industry is it the public's obligation to guarantee that there will always be a bonanza, that there will never be failure?

Of course it isn't likely to happen, mainly because there is no governmental body that could withstand the onslaught of the private powers that have vested interests in VHF. Opposition to such a plan would be led by NBC, ABC, and CBS, whose owned-and-operated stations alone are worth over a billion dollars and whose vested interest in their networking monopoly (which depends on VHF) runs many times that amount. The networks would be joined by the great station-group owners, like Westinghouse, Capital Cities, Storer, and Corinthian; by leading newspaper and magazine publishers like Post-Newsweek, Meredith, and Oklahoma Publishing; and by major newspapers in such cities as Chicago, Detroit, San Francisco, St. Louis, Milwaukee, and Buffalo, all of which own VHF stations. Even group owners of independent stations in the larger cities, like Metromedia and General Tire, would battle for their tremendously valuable franchises. What I am saying is that an attempt to take the one intelligent and simple step that could immediately solve all of our complex television problems would be met head-on by the largest aggregation of private capital ever assembled in this country, fighting to preserve the most massive total of paper values ever known to man. It is ironic that those interests are not really "vested" at all, since broadcasters don't own the franchises, they are licensed to them.

Could we not achieve a similar result through the plan called deintermixture, whereby allocations would be rearranged so that six or seven VHF stations would be clustered in a single city, as they are in New York and Los Angeles today, with six or seven UHF outlets centered in other markets, presumably those that had lost their VHF stations to make the clusters possible? Every city would be all-VHF or all-UHF. There would be no mixed markets; hence the name. The FCC toyed with this idea for a number of years and then abandoned it. They did arrange for eleven cities to be all-UHF, but, because there are only three networks and because these cities are relatively small, each one has only three UHF stations. The residents of those communities, however, get the same shows and get them just as clearly as do the viewers in other cities who watch VHF transmission.

But this idea is vulnerable to the same attack as the all-UHF plan. It would not only kill the monopoly power of the three networks but would destroy the "vested" advantage now held by station owners who not only have no real competition but are secure in the knowledge that it is impossible for any to come in.

In recent years the FCC has been looking into the feasibility of so-called "drop-ins," new VHF stations of limited power that would not interfere with the signals of existing stations. But the technologically feasible drop-ins are so few and in such small markets that the whole idea is apparently not worth any more time or effort to the FCC.

Just as the Federal Communications Commission could have solved the problem of diversity by making the country all UHF when it began its allocations, so could it have assured a multinetwork system had it parceled out its franchises on a regional basis. Instead, the commission opted to follow its radio

plan and provide for stations on a city-by-city pattern in order
to encourage local self-expression. But let us suppose the plan
had been to license all twelve VHF channels to a single large
city that is the center of a region, with no two of those centers
being so close as to cause signal interference. Each transmitter
would then have sufficient power to carry the required dis-
tance. If necessary, the signal could be amplified by booster or
satellite stations, such as those now in use in the Dakotas to
carry programs from cities like Sioux Falls and Bismarck to the
small towns of Aberdeen, Florence, Reliance, Minot, and Wil-
liston. Under such a scheme, there would be as many as twelve
and no fewer than six or eight national networks, with the remaining stations oriented to the region.

The FCC's original intention was to pursue the same localism policy for television as for radio. But television isn't radio.
Not only are there many fewer stations, but the costs of producing television programs are many times higher than radio
costs. And all independent TV stations, even the most prosperous VHFs, depend on syndicated movies, talk shows, and reruns of former network series for their basic programming.
Aside from local news and sports exhibitions, there is little regular local television production beyond a few hours a week in
the ten or twelve largest cities in the land.

More important, the commission overlooked the fact that
since most cities have only three television stations, there
would be only network affiliates to watch, which meant that at
least during prime time (and, as it has turned out, during most
of the rest of the day) all the programs would be fed out of
master control in Los Angeles or New York. As the networks
have absorbed more and more of local time, the stations have

become increasingly confined to functioning as mere outlets for the networks. Instead of producing programs, they just turn a switch.

The FCC has begun a new investigation of network activities, based on a petition by the Westinghouse stations questioning the forced abdication of local responsibility by affiliates. The petition was supported by the Office of Communications of the United Church of Christ, which emphasized "the slow but steady increase of network programming over the past decade at the inevitable expense of locally oriented programs."

The FCC is not likely to abandon its localism doctrine in favor of a regional design, or any other structure. Such a move would not only meet the same political opposition as would an all-UHF proposal, but it would be fought by the leaders of every city not selected as a regional center.

It is possible to improve television programming even without changing existing channel allocations or opening television up to many networks. Though these reforms may be politically difficult or even impossible to attain, they are worth attention.

One such idea was an outgrowth of the "50-50 plan" set forth by the FCC Study Committee in 1966. It stipulated that no network could own, either by production or purchase, more than 50 percent of its prime-time programming. This proposal was obviously a compromise of the conflicting views of committee members, and like many such adjustments it satisfied none of the businessmen who would have to live with it, and it died aborning.

Let us suppose a 0:100 ratio instead of the 50-50 plan. This would mean the network could neither produce nor buy any program; it could only sell time. The network would be treated like a railroad, bus line, or telephone company in that it would be required by law to sell its product to all comers at previously published rates—in short, the network would be treated like a common carrier. The producer would pay the aggregate of the time charges of the affiliated stations, and this price would have nothing to do with the size or composition of the audience that the show might get. The producer would then sell sponsorship or announcements to advertisers. The reverse arrangement could also work: the advertiser might buy a full time period from the network and then purchase the program from the producer.

Such a plan would correct some of the economic imbalance inherent in the industry's bargaining relationships, but it would not completely solve the problem of diversity in programming. There would probably still be the push for the largest audience, of women eighteen to forty-nine, though there would also be some exceptions (as there were in the days when advertisers controlled all shows). Also, with regulated and published time rates, competition between networks and stations for dollars based on rating points would disappear. The flow-of-audience theory would no longer apply, because with only three networks, the advertisers' demand for time would continue to exceed the networks' supply, and a network would not be harmed if it scheduled a relatively low-rating program or a program that appealed to older people. In any event, the network could not legally refuse to run an otherwise acceptable program simply because of an unsatisfactory rating potential. The common-carrier idea wouldn't do the whole job, but it would help.

In their book *Television Economics* Bruce Owen, Jack

Beebe, and Willard Manning are not only partial to the "common carrier" idea, but have come up with two other ingenious plans. One is to have a different network control the facilities now used by ABC or NBC or CBS each day of the week. This would result in twenty-one networks, with the advantage that program selection would be made by what one presumes might be twenty-one different points of view. I doubt this method would be of much help. It would give a producer more customers, each with a proportionately smaller program requirement, but it would not remove the barriers to diversity, for we would still face the quest for the lowest common denominator with the desired demographics, and we would not be rid of the flow-of-audience bugaboo.

Their other proposal is more attractive. Borrowing from the English model, where a single commercial licensee is granted rights in certain cities on certain days, they suggest giving one network access to the affiliates of all three existing chains for specified time periods. That might well be modified by giving one network the right to program all of the ABC, NBC, and CBS affiliates on one day each week, a total of seven networks, each of which would run on three tracks. This scheme would not cure the economic inequities, but it would strike a blow for program diversity.

The network of the day would devote one of its sets of affiliates rather than all three sets to attracting the largest mass audience. It would take pains not to fractionalize that major audience. Competing only with itself, it would program its other two chains of stations to pick up two other types of viewer, each group perhaps smaller in total than the first, but each embracing people in different categories of age, sex, education, interests, and the like. Instead of striving for a little better than one-third of the largest audience, the way CBS, NBC, and ABC do now, the new network would get all of that group plus two other audiences as yet untapped. Its economic self-interest would dictate that it try to attract the largest overall total of viewers possible.

This not only sounds like a good idea, but might be attainable. Assuming ABC, CBS, and NBC would oppose any threat to their domains, the essence of the plan might be salvaged by turning it over to them. Thus ABC might be the single network on Mondays and Thursdays, CBS on Tuesdays and Fridays, and NBC on Wednesdays and Saturdays. All three networks could continue to program Sundays as they do now.

There are simpler reforms that can be legislated by the FCC. First of all, the commission can amend the Prime-Time Access Rule to give it greater force and meaning. We have already suggested in a previous chapter a basic change that might be made, including checkerboarding the access slots throughout prime time with different networks having different times so syndicated programs can confront network programs.

There is a common belief that syndicated shows cannot successfully compete with network fare because distribution takes so much of the producer's dollar that there is not enough left to match the network's expenditure on production. While it is true that the cost of selling on a station-by-station basis is high, it is a mistake to believe that selling to a network is free. Companies that produce shows for network exhibition maintain scores of vice-presidents and lesser officers who devote themselves to constant meetings, travel, and entertainment, first to find out what a network wants, then to convince it that the producer has the desired property, next to keep the buyer satisfied during the process of production, and finally to persuade it to exercise options, such as picking up a pilot or renewing a series. Often there is a sales agent involved, who traditionally is paid in perpetuity 10 percent of all the gross monies received from the show—a sum which in itself approaches the cost of syndicated distribution. The difference is that the network producer buries all this in his books as part of "production cost."

The syndicator can take advantage of economies in production that are not open to the network producer. The syndicator is master of his own fate. He knows he's going to make twenty-six episodes of his series and can amortize his fixed overall costs accordingly. But the network producer gets an order for only thirteen episodes, and he isn't sure about those. As a result, he has to pay more than the syndicator for comparable actors, writers, and directors.

The new popularity of what the critics call the "second season" doesn't affect the syndicator, but it is devastating to the network producer. Today this concept has gone so far that by the end of the first week of December 1976 more than half the prime-time series introduced by the networks the previous September had been canceled. By the end of March 1977 some of the "second season" series were replaced by "third season" entries. The same pattern was followed during the ensuing year. On October 2, 1978, a new record was established: on that day NBC announced the cancellation of a series that was exactly two weeks old.

There are a number of reasons for this high mortality rate, first of which is the increased use of tape. The time lapse from script writing to the delivery of the print of a filmed episode is between ten and twelve weeks, but this period is cut in half when tape is used, so that a sudden cancellation results in destruction of much less unfinished material—that is, there are fewer partially or completely finished episodes that will never see the light of day and must be classified as a dead loss. Secondly, the rating services have developed electronic reporting systems that reveal the ratings of any particular program twenty-four hours after broadcast rather than two weeks later as was formerly the case. This development has made it easier for the network hatchet-wielders to confirm that a show's ratings are consistently disastrous within a few weeks of its debut. But perhaps the most important reason for the quick disposal of a series is that the rise of ABC to first place in the ratings race (prior to 1976 it had been consistently last) has intensified competition: the financial risk in having a poorly rated show in the early part of prime time is so huge that no network can allow it to continue for long. Despite the heavy cost of quick turnovers and the forced substitution of expensive "blockbuster" movies or specials, the network must literally "buy" an audience in self-defense.

Now that they face the increased risk of early cancellation, many of the producers who traditionally sold programs only to networks have turned to syndication as an outlet for their wares. But even in syndication they must contract with one of the network owned-and-operated station groups in order to bring a series to life. The FCC could change this by prohibiting prime-time stripping by independent stations, thus forcing them into the market for one-per-week series, but this would penalize the underdog, who has a hard enough time competing with the network stations as it is. Another remedy would be to prohibit the networks from owning stations. Such a move would infuriate the networks probably more than any other proposal, but, as we have already noted, there is no more necessity for the networks to own stations than there was for them to be in the syndication business. A bill on file in the House of Representatives would prevent ownership by a network of more than one station. It probably won't pass, but there is no sound economic or social reason why it shouldn't.

One other change should be made in the Prime-Time Access Rule, regarding the 1971 provision which prohibited the networks from exacting a net profit participation from producers. Vast sums of money are still being paid by producers to the networks for profit arrangements that were made before the rule was passed. If the profit snatching is wrong now, it was wrong in the past. The networks should be ordered to return their ill-gotten gains, or at least to stop their continued collection under old contracts.

Aside from the access rule, the FCC could help to achieve more balanced programming by simply directing each network to schedule an hour or two during weekly prime time of unsponsored, or what in radio parlance was called sustaining, material. Because of the networks' anxiety about flow of audience, such shows should probably be transmitted during the last hour of prime time. To avoid the creation of a ghetto, the three networks should schedule them on different nights. It would, of course, also be necessary to prohibit the affiliated stations from preempting them with local commercial programs. There would be no preemption except for other noncommercial broadcasts. In light of the swollen profits of the networks and the stations, there would be no financial problems.

This idea is not a novel one. In 1946, when radio reigned,

the FCC published the "Blue Book," in which it listed "the public service responsibilities of broadcast licensees." The FCC would consider four matters in the granting and renewal of licenses: the carrying of "sustaining" programming in order "to provide a balanced program structure," the use of local live talent programs, the broadcast of programs concerning important public issues, and the elimination of advertising excesses.

The Blue Book explained that there were five purposes in requiring "sustaining" programming. The first was to achieve "balance." The second was to encourage programs that by their nature were not proper for sponsorship, such as those under the direction of religious, educational, government, or social welfare groups. The third purpose was to serve such minority interests as classical music or drama. The fourth was to serve the needs of nonprofit organizations, such as educational institutions. And, finally, such programming would provide room for experimental shows that might not at the time be safe enough for the ordinary advertiser.

Radio broadcasters greeted these rules with howls of indignation, and they were not enforced beyond the reprimand stage. But the FCC never repudiated the Blue Book standards and there is no reason why it should not now take steps to institute them.

Periodically the FCC is asked to limit reruns on the network during prime time. The agitation stems in large part from the Hollywood unions, who believe that there would be more employment for their members if reruns were limited. Originally, television operated under a plan whereby 39 episodes of a series were filmed and 13 were repeated, for a ratio of 3:1. When the number of initial episodes fell by degrees down to 26, the ratio became 1:1 and the unions petitioned to move it back to 3:1. Today a maximum of 22 episodes are ordered for most series, which means that unless there are either 8 preemptions or 8 segments of a summer replacement, at least some of the episodes will be repeated more than once. Some people find this offensive. Paul Klein, writing in *New York* magazine, described CBS running repeats of the hour-long Jackie Gleason "Honeymooners" series. "These are actually repeats of repeats," he said, "the foremost example of Future Shlock to date. Future Shlock is the repeating, in prime time, in midseason, of those programs you hated in the past."

10

Alternative Sources: Cable, Pay TV, and Public TV

"The cable industry has been long on promise. You have called yourself a medium of choice, but you very often have only provided an echo. Even the new pay services which feature movies are an extended version of the networks' night at the movies—without commercials. Are these services so distinctive that you can hope to expand your base of 1.6 million pay subscribers to reach millions more?"
— FCC chairman Charles Ferris to the convention of the National Cable Television Organization in New Orleans, May 7, 1978

The strongest alternatives to commercial television are cable television and pay television. The two have recently been tied together for general consideration, although pay TV, unlike cable, can come over the airwaves. In the early 1970s the marketers of a cable connection began to offer customers, on a subscription basis, the promise of eventual channels that would carry new movies and other desirable entertainment free of advertising.

Initially, cable television was called Community Antenna Television. TV signals travel in a straight line, and anything that obstructs their passage, be it buildings in New York or mountains in Colorado, causes a reception problem. The first cable systems were started in small valley towns in Pennsylvania. TV signals passed untapped over these towns until the late 1940s when an enterprising citizen named Robert Tarlton put an antenna atop Panther Mountain and then ran a wire down to homes in nearby Lansford, carrying television signals from Philadelphia, just sixty-five miles away. Tarlton had created the first community antenna television system. Soon the Pennsylvania mountain country was dotted with small cable companies, many of them cooperative ventures of the residents of small towns. But it wasn't long before business entrepreneurs learned that a five-dollar subscription fee for a month's cable service could be a steady source of income. And a cable system required very little management once it was started, the major task being to collect the bills.

As long as the cable schemes were restricted to places unable to receive any other signals, the rest of the television industry ignored them. Not until cable systems were established in towns that had a television station and threatened to dilute that station's audience did broadcasters and producers express concern. Even then no serious alarm was sounded, because the early cable systems covered so few homes. I remember the day in 1955 when a salesman for the Ziv Company (a leading film syndicator) called his home office in New York to report that he was unable to sell "Cisco Kid" in Reno (at that time a one-station town) because the manager said the series was being piped into Reno on a community antenna system, having been picked up from a San Francisco transmitter. He got some fast advice: Since the cable went into only two hundred homes and the television station at that time could reach twenty thousand homes, the salesman should go back to the station manager and offer to cut the price of the series by the equivalent of 1 percent. He did; the manager saw the point, joined in the laugh, and bought the show.

By the mid-1960s cable was no laughing matter to syndicators or to broadcasters. It was becoming a respectable business, claiming 2 million homes and 6 million viewers. Mayors and governing boards in some of America's largest municipalities were being pressured by well-financed lobbies to permit the wiring of their cities. The cable owners' associations, extrapolating from recent years' experience, predicted a growth rate that promised national saturation by the 1980s.

Broadcasters rushed to their friends at the FCC, who obliged by freezing cable expansion in the top cities. They also prohibited cable from bringing in "distant signals," programs piped into three-station markets from independent stations located in nonadjacent cities. The station owners complained that cable systems would dilute or "fractionalize" their audience, and that the cable operator was a competitor who had sneaked in by a shortcut and bore none of the costs and restrictions that beset broadcasters.

But it was syndicators who took their grievance to the courts. The cable systems, they said, were making it impossible for them to sell their programs in some cities and seriously depressing the prices in others. The fundamental inequity was that the cable people simply took their shows off the air without paying for them, while their competitors, the stations, had to buy their broadcast rights. This was piracy, said the syndicators, and they asked for relief under the copyright law. The association of cable owners replied that they weren't broadcasters, that they just put up an antenna, received a signal, amplified it, and sent it by wire to subscribers—something akin to what happens when the owner of a large apartment house or hotel puts a single antenna on the roof of his building and pipes the signals into individual rooms. The Supreme Court agreed with the cable view.

A decade of disputes was finally settled on October 29, 1976, when President Ford signed the new copyright act, replacing a law that had resisted serious change since 1909. Under the new statute, a small portion of the cable operators' revenues is divided among those who own the copyrights of all programs carried on the wire. This amount is based on a complicated formula that fixes as a minimum 6.75 tenths of 1 percent of the gross monies collected from cable subscribers, against varying percentages in the same range payable for each "distant signal" that the cable carries. Lower rates are prescribed for small cable systems. Programs which run on a national network or originate from a station located in the same city area as the cable system are not paid for; presumably they could be picked up by the subscriber even without cable. The result is that the program producers and syndicators will probably get the lion's share of a relatively small sum, with the remainder going to stations that originate their own material and to composers and publishers of copyrighted music that finds the same outlet.

In the United States today there are about 13 million homes with cable TV, or about 35 million viewers. This comprises 4,000 systems serving 9,000 communities. The average system has 3,000 subscribers, but the sizes vary from the smallest with fewer than 100, to the largest, San Diego, with 57,000. The total revenues in 1977 added up to almost $1 billion, whereas the cost of laying the cable varied from a low of $4,000 per mile to $100,000 for underground construction in the largest cities. The fantastic growth pattern predicted ten years ago has not materialized, although once again the business is on an upswing. The cable industry went through a depression beginning in 1973, the combined result of that year's dispirited economy, the sharply rising costs of cable construction, and a dramatic disappearance of demand.

By 1975 the cable industry was once again prospering, mainly because of the addition of a new, attractive element—pay television. Cable technology had already advanced to where it could provide multiple channels, twenty-eight usually being the number offered to new subscribers. Today one or two of those channels are sold as optionals. They can be obtained by paying a monthly fee in addition to the regular subscription cost, and provide the viewer with access to recent motion-picture releases without commercial interruption.

There are about a dozen firms in the country supplying pay-TV programming to cable systems, the two major companies being Home Box Office, a subsidiary of Time, Inc., and Showtime, which is owned by Viacom. There have also been renewed experiments with over-the-air pay television. A decoding device is connected to the homeowner's TV set, enabling him to unscramble a jumbled picture broadcast by a local UHF transmitter. This technique was first tested fifteen years ago in such disparate markets as Hartford, Connecticut, and Etobicoke, Ontario (a Toronto suburb). Its failure at that time was due to a chicken-or-egg dilemma: subscribers would not pay for programs unless they were unusually attractive, and the suppliers couldn't buy attractive shows unless the subscribers gave them the money to pay for them.

It may well be that pay TV is the wave of the future. To its programmers men from ages seventy-five to one hundred will be just as desirable as women eighteen to forty-nine—all they have to do is to cast their votes with a monthly check.

The drawback to pay television is simply that it will require the viewing public to pay for much entertainment that it now gets free. Not only do we live in an economy of limited channels, we live in a world of limited talent, the best of which often goes where there is the most money. As the number of customers for pay TV increases, so does the amount of money available for the production of programs designed for pay television. These sums will be much larger than the amount now spent by advertisers, and pay-TV producers will eventually be able to outbid other television companies for the services of actors, writers, and directors now working in the free medium. Pay-TV subscribers will then get programs similar to those they now get without payment, and the future free television shows, having been made by inferior talent, will be worse than they are now.

We must not fall into the trap of believing that "free television" really isn't free because it carries commercials that are paid for by the viewer. There is a theory that the advertiser must get more money for his product in order to pay for his televised blurbs, which in turn raises the price which the consumer-viewer must pay for that product. But it is probably not true that the price of the product must go up because of the advertising. Even if it were, the TV viewer is not required to pay the cost. Suppose the viewer doesn't buy the product, and suppose that somebody who never watches television does buy it—the program is therefore free to the viewer, the cost being paid by his fellow citizen who ignores the tube.

More to the point, there is little basis for the belief that advertising increases the price of the advertised product. If it did, advertised items would cost more than unadvertised items, people would buy the cheaper of the two, and the effect of advertising would be contrary to its intent. The object of advertising is to increase profits through greater volume, and to stimulate consumption of the product in general and of the brand being advertised in particular. Failure to advertise will reduce the volume of sales so that the price of each unit must rise in an amount at least equal to the cost of the advertising, and presumably more. In this respect, advertising is like rent: a merchant will spend tremendous sums to have his store at the prime corner of a central city where traffic is heavy, and he will even give up much of his expensive ground-floor space in order to have alluring show windows that will attract that traffic through his doors. Yet this does not mean he must get more dollars per unit for his product than the rival tradesman who sells from a third-floor walk-up loft in a rundown part of the city. My father was a merchant who sold fur coats from an attractively appointed shop located on the most expensive corner in town. He once explained to me that "it's not rent per square foot that counts; it's rent *per coat.*"

And so with television advertising. If the commercials go off the air (as did cigarette ads a few years ago), the seller either puts his money into newspapers, magazines, billboards, and the equivalent of higher rent and attractive show windows, or his loss in volume raises his unit price by at least as much as he has saved. The result is that commercial television is just about as free monetarily to the viewer as anything he can get in our economy.

The problem of whether legislators ought to encourage or discourage pay TV thus becomes a political one. Viewers who can afford the Home Box Office type of system will benefit from the advantages of more balanced and diversified programming, whereas those who are unable to pay the required additional fees will be relegated to cheaper and second-rate material.

The FCC tried to help the networks and other broadcasters by prohibiting pay channels from running certain programs—specifically, movies that were more than three and less than ten years old, any series programs, and sports events that had consistently appeared on commercial TV. The pay and cable interests sued to enjoin the continued operation of this rule, claiming that the FCC had not only exceeded its authority in dictating an entertainment format, but had violated their constitutional rights.

On March 25, 1977, the United States Court of Appeals for the District of Columbia agreed with them, and reprimanded the FCC for the many private meetings its members had had with representatives of the affected groups during the decision-making process. In response to the commission's argument that it was merely trying to prevent the siphoning off into pay channels of the more attractive material that viewers had been getting free, the court replied that this form of protectionism was premature. It said that the FCC had failed to "put itself into a position to know whether the alleged siphoning phenomenon is a real or merely a fanciful threat to those not served by cable."

A myriad of new and wonderful technological developments are promised for the cable system of the future. They include two-way communication, direct academic testing and poll taking by means of pressing multiple-choice buttons, and an arrangement whereby sixty channels can be sent into a home over the same cable used by the telephone company. The irony of this development is that with the great cost of using the old-fashioned technology of stringing wires as opposed to the more modern electronic devices, the full use of cable will probably give us no more than would a television system using all seventy UHF channels, or even the simple remedy of deintermixture.

Another alternative to the networks' monopoly is public television, which should be able to supply programming for some of the many groups ignored by commercial broadcasters. To some extent it does, as witness its broadcasts of opera, dance, "Sesame Street" for children, and "Over Easy" for people over fifty-five. The size of its audience, however, is disappointingly small, usually ranging from 2 or 3 to a top of 10 percent of commercial television's.

One reason for this is that commercial networks and stations promote their shows and advertise themselves to an extent that is impossible for public broadcasters. Another reason is the lack of good transmitting facilities; only 85 of the 260 public broadcasting stations are in the VHF spectrum, and most of those are in small towns and college communities. More than two-thirds of the public television outlets are UHF stations, as compared with less than 15 percent of commercial stations. In the Los Angeles area, for example, there are four public broadcasting stations, all of them UHF. An organization called the Committee to Eliminate the UHF Handicap on Public Television in Los Angeles has been formed to have the FCC allocate one of the seven commercial channels for public use, an endeavor that is supported by the National Black Media Coalition. They argue that operating KCET, the major Los Angeles public station, is a "rather futile endeavor" and that the station "cannot expect to reach the widest possible audience until it is transferred to a VHF frequency." Their chances of acquiring a

VHF station are slim. A decade ago it was rumored that one of the four independent VHF stations in Los Angeles was for sale. The other six commercial broadcasters quickly pledged substantial financial contributions to the local public television people, hoping that they would buy the station and thus reduce the commercial competition, precisely what had happened in New York City several years before. But the commercial station was not put up for sale then and there is no indication of its happening soon.

Perhaps the most significant reason why public television's ratings do not approach those of the commercial stations is that the production of the programs simply isn't good enough to attract the audience that demands the professional pacing and polish of commercial programs but is dissatisfied with their subject matter. Public television does not have the tremendous sums of money needed to produce full-time programming of the technical excellence that American viewers have learned to expect.

The problem of funding public broadcasting has always presented a dilemma for a democratic society: how do we prevent the government which finances a medium of communication from using it for political purposes? In the beginning, American public broadcasting, or "educational television" as it was then called, was financed almost entirely by the Ford Foundation, a private charitable organization. The decision on the part of the Ford Foundation to withdraw its support gradually resulted in the passage of the Public Broadcasting Act of 1967. This legislation established a national apparatus headed by the Corporation for Public Broadcasting, which was designed to channel a modest amount of federal funds into the system. The Public Broadcasting Service was set up as a programming agency for the group of some 260 public stations, although each station retained its autonomy. PBS lacked both the power and the persuasiveness of a commercial network and the amount of money made available to it was far less than what advertisers pay to a commercial network for programming. To cope with the financial problem, the more enterprising public television stations moved in two directions: they sought to obtain more money, and they sought to obtain cheaper programming.

But the methods the public stations adopted to raise money opened them to the charge that they had become too commercial. First they sought out grants from large advertisers, who would use public television to improve their corporate image. Under this arrangement, the benefactor is not allowed a full commercial announcement in the show, but his philanthropy is acknowledged and his logo is displayed. Most important, he takes out newspaper and magazine advertisements and even publicizes his involvement in announcements on commercial television. All of this investment is made for the ostensible purpose of urging a large audience to tune in to a "culturally broadening" program. Some commercial broadcasters have expressed unhappiness with what are clearly self-serving motives. On the other hand, a low-rating competitor such as public broadcasting weakens the pressures commercial broadcasters might feel to run a lot of unprofitable public-service programming.

Another method of raising funds is direct solicitation of viewers. Intermissions between acts of plays and operas are utilized for pleas to the viewers to send financial contributions. These pitches are not of the 30-second or 1-minute commercial variety but go on for 5 or 10 minutes at a time. WNET, the public broadcasting station in New York City, manages to collect over $5 million annually from approximately 300,000 subscribers. But this is an expensive business; the WNET operating budget is higher than that of any commercial station in the city, despite the fact that its locally produced programs add up to no more than fourteen hours each week. Although commercial stations hire advertising salesmen, they do not have to engage in the far more costly chore of fund raising.

The business of raising money through grants and subscriptions has affected the type of programming produced by the public stations. These stations have been criticized for their failure properly to serve ethnic and economic minorities. New York's WNET, for example, no longer produces a black or Hispanic series. Instead, it specializes in programs like "Live from Lincoln Center," and subscribes to series like "Masterpiece Theatre," both of which appeal to the tastes of viewers in the economic bracket most likely to contribute money. At the same time, these viewers attract well-heeled underwriters who are anxious to convince the public that they are interested in cultural uplift as well as profit. Thus, a booklet distributed by WNET to corporations points out that "public television is cherished by underwriters because it includes America's most influential citizens—the active, the aware, the movers and shapers of society."

Michael Rice, former general manager of WGBH, the public broadcasting station in Boston, has said: "We are putting as much effort into selling our proposals as into creating them. Managers are known as much—or more—for their grantsmanship as they are for the programs that come out of it."

The reverse side of the economic problem is how to get better programming for less money. For the time being, at least, the Public Broadcasting Service has found a partial solution in the purchase of successful British productions. It is unrealistic to expect public broadcasting to be able to afford the $10 million price tag usually placed on an American-made series of twenty-two one-hour programs. Such "Masterpiece Theatre," series as "Upstairs Downstairs" and "Poldark," and the British Broadcasting Corporation's productions of Shakespeare, have given American public broadcasting viewers top-notch productions at prices far lower than would be paid for the comparable American product, because whatever the cost, it has presumably been met in England and other parts of the world. Whatever is paid by PBS to the producers of these British programs is "gravy"—and it is more than would otherwise have been obtainable from American television. This is because all of these productions had been or certainly would be turned down by our commercial networks because of their belief (one that is supported by many years of experience) that only a small proportion of the American audience will watch programs in which actors speak with a British accent.

This emphasis on British programming has caused complaints from citizens who have argued that the money of American taxpayers should be spent to encourage American talent, creativity, and production. Early in 1978, Sanford Wolff, national executive secretary of the American Federation of Television and Radio Artists, told the House Subcommittee on Communications that "the assignment of large blocks of prime time to foreign-made acquisitions militates against the encouragement of new independent producers and productions in the United States. We are a large country, blessed with a multitude of creative people who need opportunities to grow and serve the public. Unfortunately, such opportunities are increasingly closed off to them abroad, as most of the English-speaking world erects increasingly stringent barriers and quotas against American programs. We do not believe that public broadcasting was created to make this situation worse. We do believe that it was created, at least in part, to encourage American creative talent in the media. With upwards of 23 percent of prime time usurped by foreign product, public broadcasting is not fully addressing its purpose." And a woman named Ellen Stern Harris of Los Angeles told the same committee, "California was never a British Colony, but my children think it is."

David Ives of the WGBH (Boston) Educational Foundation responded to this criticism in a letter published in *Newsweek* September 25, 1978. After agreeing that there should be a U.S. version of "Masterpiece Theatre," he said: "The problem, as always, is money. We are currently finishing location shooting of 'The Scarlet Letter,' planned for airing on PBS next Spring. But it took us two and a half years to find the funds for it—some $2,250,000—and even that is proving to be frighteningly tight. That amount is only a little less than the cost of an entire season of 'Masterpiece Theatre' to Mobil. Public television won't have its domestic version no matter how good the idea, until we find much greater funds from some place."

The solution to the economic problem may be forthcoming in the "rewrite" of the Communications Act that has been proposed by the House Subcommittee on Communications under the chairmanship of Congressman Lionel Van Deerlin. The key revision in this proposal, which was to go before Congress for initial consideration sometime in 1979, requires commercial television stations to pay a fee to the federal government for the right to use the airwaves, a portion of which would be diverted for the support of public broadcasting. There were differences of opinion among the members of the subcommittee as to how much, if any, of this money is to be used for public television, differences which pretty much follow party lines.

And it is these differences—whether, for instance, government funding of public television would turn it into an organ of political and cultural propaganda—that must be resolved before any such proposal becomes law.

The Van Deerlin rewrite would in effect charge commercial television with the duty of supporting public television by this indirect license-fee method. Should it not succeed, further consideration could be given to the possibility of requiring commercial broadcasters to take over the functions of public TV—at their expense. Remembering that more than thirty years ago the FCC Blue Book suggested that one of the requisites of licensing a commercial broadcaster be the transmission of "sustaining" programs that would serve minority tastes and interests, it would appear that the money and effort currently expended on public TV might well be devoted to FCC enforcement of those standards. Not only prestige and pride, but the desire to keep viewers tuned to their stations might operate to create network competition for excellence of these programs. In other words, there might be superior public television on commercial TV stations for at least a few hours each week.

11

The Roads to Relief:
The FCC, Congress,
and the Courts

"The FCC for over thirty years has an all but unblemished record of misconceiving both the problems and the available remedies in broadcasting. That they have done so with the best of intentions and (except for a few sordid interludes) with high standards of integrity, is a real source of scandal."
— Professor Peter O. Steiner, University of Wisconsin Department of
Economics

To what extent should corporate managers tailor their business practices to the demands of civilized society—knowing that their altruism will be at the expense of their stockholders? Should the management of an oil company, for example, refrain from drilling a potentially prosperous oil well in a recreational bay area because of the danger of spills? Or should it take the position that ecological questions are matters of opinion about national priorities, and who is the manager to place his personal views above the claims of the stockholders who pay his salary and trust him to protect their economic interests? Should a union leader tell his members that wage increases at this time are inflationary, and that they should forgo demanding the pay raise that they elected him to get for them? What would happen to him if he took such a position?

The resolutions of controversial issues, such as control of inflation and conservation of ecological resources, are indeed matters of public policy. Under an economic system based in theory on competitive free enterprise, we cannot expect such anxieties to be given priority by private corporate management. They are, instead, the concern of all the people, and the people must act through their government. If this points in the direction of more "government intereference in business," chalk it up as another cost of industrial development.

With most American industry, the battle between private and public interest is first settled in favor of private interest. The public must await the outcome of the slow process of legislation, the creation of effective administrative machinery, and the winning of court tests. But in the television industry there is theoretically no reason for these problems or delays. Television profits depend upon utilization of the public's property, the airwaves, and all stations are subject to having their right to continue to use these channels examined every three years by an agency of the United States. Even though the FCC has never denied renewal of such a license because of complaints about a television station's programming, and has shown little enthusiasm for performing many other regulatory functions, we should not eliminate it from consideration as a potential source of meaningful reform.

Since 1953, when the industry was seven years old, there have been continuous investigations by both branches of Congress, constant examination by the FCC's Special Network

Study Committee and its successor study group, and an ongoing probe by the antitrust division of the Department of Justice. These inquiries, many of which took place at the same time and overlapped each other, have concentrated on the anticompetitive aspects of the network practices, on how they affect advertisers in general and small businesses in particular, on what they do to program producers and to broadcasters, and the effect of network television on the public, with special emphasis on children and teen-agers.

These extensive investigations brought forth no meaningful legislation until the Prime-Time Access Rule was enacted in 1971. What is most significant is the fact that the changes finally made by the rule had been proposed at investigatory hearings seventeen years before the rule was promulgated, and some aspects of it were recommended by congressional committee reports as long as fifteen years before 1971.

Starting in 1955, the FCC conducted one of the longest investigations of the television industry on record. It appointed Roscoe L. Barrow, dean of the University of Cincinnati Law School, to "study every possible facet of the network business." Barrow reported within two years and went back to his university, but his chief counsel, Ashbrook Bryant, stayed on and continued the investigation as head of a newly created Office of Network Study. Bryant, a great-grandson of William Cullen Bryant, displayed remarkable powers of endurance and tenacity. He continued the investigation for eight years, much of which time was spent in taking testimony from practically every man and woman connected with the industry. The "Bryant Report" of 1965 became the basis for an FCC proposal that networks get out of the syndication business and stop exacting profit participation from producers, recommendations that were finally enacted five years later. In addition, the report recommended that networks not be permitted either to produce or buy more than half the programs that they run in prime time.

One may well wonder why the many investigations produced no other action than the mild prime-time-access reform. And why did it take fifteen years to accomplish that? The two network practices prohibited by the access rule (exaction of a profit share and of syndication rights) were never endorsed as good or necessary during the course of those investigations. Of course there were many spokesmen who gave excuses for those incursions, but in all the thousands of pages of testimony it is hard to find a witness who said that the industry could not flourish without them.

The members of the FCC are appointed by the President with the advice and consent of the Senate and serve for a seven-year term. The terms are staggered so that an appointment is made every year. With three or four exceptions, they have been men. Most of them have been lawyers, although some have been appointed from executive positions in the communications industry. Some have been lame-duck congressmen, others counsel for congressmen, various investigative committees, and other administrative agencies. For the most part they have been an undistinguished group who have not been disposed to look kindly on any suggestion that would upset the status quo of a prosperous industry. There have been outstanding exceptions, but because there are seven members on the commission, these men and women have been known as dissenters when they are polite and troublemakers when they aren't.

In summary, the FCC is a regulatory agency made up of people who don't want to regulate. Thus, Dean Burch, a recent chairman of the FCC, was an implacable opponent of the Prime-Time Access Rule, partly because, as he put it, he was opposed to regulation and preferred "free enterprise." Commissioner Robert E. Lee began his term saying, "I don't believe in government regulations." George McConnaughy, an earlier chairman, said he believed in "as few controls as possible," while John Doerfer, who followed him as chairman, told a congressional committee: "Competition does not frighten me. If the competitive principles of this country do not take care of that situation, then we are hopelessly sunk." It was Doerfer who while testifying before the House Antitrust Subcommittee exhibited a fine pronetwork bias. The committee counsel had just read the conclusion of a radio study which said that the network organizations were dominant "at every turn" in the radio industry.

COUNSEL: Would that be a matter that would be disturbing to you if the same situation were shown in television broadcasting?
DOERFER: Not at all.
COUNSEL: It would not disturb you?
DOERFER: Not at all.
COUNSEL: Explain why not.
DOERFER: Somebody has to be dominant. Somebody is big.

The pity is that these men apparently never understood that the FCC was brought into existence to regulate, that there is no such thing as free enterprise in an unrestrained communications industry, that laissez-faire is inadequate to resolve such abuses as those brought about by the network monopoly—in short, that regulation does not destroy competition here, but must be enforced to make competition possible.

Professor Bernard Schwartz was forced to resign as counsel to the House Oversight Committee after he had publicized, over the objections of some of the committee members, findings that were critical of the Federal Communications Commission. (The controversial material had to do with certain commissioners charging the government for the expenses of convention and meeting trips that were also paid by various branches of the television industry, and also continual fraternization with executives of companies appearing as litigants before the commission, including acceptance of various sorts of lavish entertainment.) After he left the oversight committee, Schwartz published a book entitled *The Professor and the Commissions*, in which he wrote the following: "A prime characteristic of the regulatory commission in its ossified stage is that it is staffed by men who are basically out of sympathy with the regulatory objectives which the agency was created to accomplish. In none of the regulatory agencies has this been more apparent than in the FCC."

The members of the FCC are not oblivious to the criticism leveled at them for what appears to be a proindustry bias. In 1973 the late Congressman Torbert McDonald of Massachusetts, chairman of the House Subcommittee on Communications, blew up at a public hearing at which members of the commission were present. He said that he couldn't understand the frenzy of broadcasters to obtain passage of the bill that would extend their license period from three to five years, when they have "a motherly FCC" taking care of them, and he referred to a recent case where "a station can promise anything, fulfill none of its promises, and still get a renewal." He concluded: "A guy has to try, to really *want* to lose his license."

The dereliction has been discussed in open hearing among the commissioners themselves. Former commissioner Nicholas Johnson put himself on record: "The policy of the Commission is clear. The incumbent will win unless his behavior is so bad that we would be forced to take away the license even if there were no competing applications." To which statement, Chairman Dean Burch, who seldom agreed with Johnson on anything, replied, "Yes, the industry has become a bit insular, a bit self-conscious. . . ."

It is easy to say that the FCC, like other regulatory agencies, has become a captive of the business it was created to supervise. Owen, Beebe, and Manning take a somewhat different view. In their opinion "The FCC has been uncomfortable with the notion that its policies have economic implications and indeed with the notion that broadcasting is a business. The quasi-official view of broadcasting at the FCC has been that broadcasters are public-spirited citizens, fiduciaries of the public, who are unfortunately obliged to sell advertising in order to defray expenses of operation. The responsibility of broadcasters is, officially, to the viewing public, and not to the shareholders. This unrealistic view is the source of . . . much ineffective policy."

I find it hard to agree with their appraisal. Commissioners I have known are hard-headed men who understand the economic realities, men who are too cynical to regard broadcasters as "public-spirited citizens." I agree that they are "uncomfortable," but I think that is because they are aware of their power and are afraid to use it.

Nowhere is this more evident than in their handling of challenges to television station license renewals. Without preparation these people have been catapulted into a position where they must constantly make decisions as to renewals and grants that can mean enormous gains or losses for their petitioners. And these decisions are based on an extremely vague guideline. Under the statute, grants are to be made on the basis of "public interest, convenience, and necessity," words subject to many interpretations.

A prime example of how important and how difficult these interpretations can be occurred in late 1977 in connection with a renewal application filed by the Cowles Broadcasting Company for station WESH-TV, in Daytona Beach, Florida. The Cowles renewal was challenged by a local group on the grounds that Cowles owns a number of other stations; there is a well-established FCC guideline to the effect that in any such case local ownership should be preferred. The challengers also pointed out that Cowles's performance in Daytona Beach had been less than satisfactory.

The commission was divided. All members agreed that the challenger was entitled to a "clear preference" because Cowles is a chain owner, but the majority ruled in favor of Cowles because, it said, it had demonstrated "superior" performance in the operation of the station and was thus entitled to "a plus of major significance." The majority cited a 1970 decision of the U.S. court of appeals which said that broadcasters providing "superior" services are entitled to a substantial advantage in a comparative renewal hearing. The vote was four to three.

When the commissioners learned that the challenger was appealing their decision, they felt it would be helpful to Cowles if its favorable vote was not so close. The chairman, Richard Wiley, had voted with the dissenters because, he said, he could not accept the word *superior* to describe the station's past operations. He would go along with the word *substantial*. Accordingly, the FCC met again and issued a "clarification" of its previous decision. It now stated that it had used the word *superior* to describe service that was "solid and favorable" rather than "exceptional," and it added: "We propose to use the word 'substantial' to describe the kind of performance evidenced by the WESH-TV record." The message to the industry was that broadcasters need not provide "superior" service to protect themselves against competing applicants at renewal time, but merely "substantial" service, service that is "favorable and substantially above the level of mediocrity" that might "just minimally warrant renewal." The "clarification" added that although the previous decision had stated that the challenger was entitled to a "clear preference" because of Cowles's ownership of other stations, it had not been intended to suggest any view as to *how much weight* should be attached to the preference, and the preference emerged as "of little decisional significance."

As might have been expected after this semantic legerdemain, the Washington court overturned the WESH-TV decision. On September 25, 1978, a three-judge panel told the FCC that it had acted unreasonably when it renewed the Cowles application. The court, speaking through Judge Richard Wilkey, criticized the FCC for finding favorably to the challenger on the issue of ownership diversification without "even vaguely [describing] how it aggregated its findings into the decisive balance." It said that the decision process fell "somewhere on the distant side of arbitrary," and concluded: "We do not see how performance that is merely average, whether 'solid' or not, can warrant renewal or, in fact, be of especial relevance without some finding that the challenger's performance would likely be no more satisfactory."

In another instance, renewal was denied to a television station because of an unsatisfactory programming policy, but this was done over the objections of the FCC. As the result of complaints filed by a church group and a black citizens committee in 1966, alleging that WLBT-TV in Jackson, Mississippi, had all but ignored Jackson's substantial black community in its programming and practices, the commission granted the station a renewal for only a short term. On appeal to the Circuit Court of Appeals for the District of Columbia, Justice Warren Burger, who was later to become chief justice, first held that the church and black groups were in good standing before the court despite the fact that neither of them had any pecuniary interest in the outcome of the case. He then negated the short-term renewal and ordered a hearing before the FCC. The commission obliged by holding a hearing and granting the station a full three-year renewal. When the matter again came before Burger in 1969, he vacated the FCC action and invited new applications for the frequency, with WBLT permitted to be one of those applicants. Burger predicated his decision on the statement that "the administrative conduct reflected in this record is beyond repair."

Although the WESH-TV and the WLBT-TV cases demonstrate to what lengths the commissioners will go to justify a license renewal, we must turn to a more flagrant case for a revelation of *why* the commissioners act as they do. We have already noted that the license of WPIX, New York, was challenged on the grounds that the station had falsified its news reports. In mid-June 1978 the FCC renewed this license by a four-to-three vote, the majority holding that the news distortion and inadequate supervision did not involve misdeeds of sufficient importance to warrant denial. The minority said that the station was "guilty of a seriously deficient performance . . . which demonstrates either that the station's top management during most of 1969 directly condoned the improper past news practices or that they did not want to uncover the facts about the misconduct." The minority implicitly criticized the majority by saying that WPIX's license could be renewed only "by doing extreme violence to any meaningful standard of 'sound, favorable and substantial service,'" criticism which brought forth an angry reply. Commissioner James Quello, who had voted for the renewal, said he was "appalled" by a regulatory process that places "a long-term, highly respected licensee in jeopardy through an opportunistic challenge that pits 'paper' promises versus actual long-term performance. . . . I'm especially concerned with the basic unfairness of even considering the harsh ultimate penalty of license revocation (which in this case would amount to a $75 million fine) because of a dereliction whose seriousness has been exaggerated out of context and proportion. This type of charge couldn't possibly warrant even an indictment, let alone a conviction, in a civil or criminal proceeding."

In one revealing statement we see the mental process that explains why the FCC record in challenge cases is so consistent. A "long-term" licensee is, by definition, "highly respected" no matter what he has done or failed to do in the operation of his franchise, while any challenger is by definition "opportunistic." To take away the licensee's right to use the public's property is the "harsh ultimate penalty" because it deprives him of something worth $75 million. No matter that some years ago an earlier commission entrusted this property to him free. What is important to the FCC is the assumption that the licensee "owns" the franchise, and that he shouldn't lose it unless what he has done justifies "an indictment" or a "conviction." The commissioners haven't interpreted "public interest, convenience, and necessity" as meaning "You've done a good job for the public in running your station"; they have assumed it means "You've acted within the law and are not guilty of an offense so heinous that it would justify a fine of $75 million!"

The FCC's passive and polite attitude toward the networks was epitomized in the summer of 1978 as a result of the so-called "winner-take-all" tennis matches. Approximately a year before, the CBS network had broadcast a series of matches between top tennis stars involving prize money running to a half-million dollars each. CBS promoted these matches as "winner-take-all," explaining over the air and in print that the entire prize would go to the winner and the loser would get nothing. This was untrue; in each case an arrangement had been made for division of the money. Thus, for example, in the Connors–Nastase match, it was prearranged that Connors would receive $500,000 and Nastase $150,000, regardless of the outcome.

As later testified to before the House subcommittee of the Judiciary and the FCC, certain CBS executives knew about this plan well before the promotional announcements were made. At first they claimed to have been unaware of the prepayment arrangements but admitted that "a greater effort should have been made to elicit the correct facts from the promoter." Later, before the subcommittee, Robert Wussler, CBS network president, admitted that he knew "early on" that the four matches in the CBS "Heavyweight Championship of Tennis" series had not been "winner-take-all" as advertised. He claimed that he did not sit down in a closed room and say, "How can we come up with a gimmick. . . . how can we deceive the public?" adding that it was simply "sloppy procedures." He admitted letting the deception continue throughout the series even though he knew that in the second match both players would receive $150,000 in addition to the $250,000 which would go to the winner.

The FCC also found that the CBS executives had misled the commission and hidden from it and public scrutiny, as required by law, the fact that CBS had received complimentary rooms, food, and beverages from a Las Vegas hotel in connection with one of the tennis matches.

On April 9, 1978, Gene Jankowski, president of the CBS broadcast group, appeared on the CBS television network to apologize to the public for the tennis deception. He said it wouldn't happen again. Two weeks later he officially told the same thing to the FCC. Meanwhile, Wussler had been demoted to his previous position as chief of the CBS sports division, shortly after which he announced his "resignation" from CBS.

Nevertheless, the FCC decided to punish the network. The CBS-owned-and-operated television station in Los Angeles, KNXT, was up for renewal. The FCC renewed its license, but for only one year rather than the usual three.

While it may appear that this action is but a "slap on the wrist" and that the FCC is in effect saying that deceit of the public and of the United States government is not a sufficient offense to result in refusal to renew a license, it is nevertheless significant that for the first time in television history there has been a suggestion that the license of a network-owned-and-operated station is not sacrosanct. This may reflect the influence of the new commissioners appointed by President Carter. It is noteworthy that the vote in the WPIX decision was four to three and the dissenters were Carter-appointed "rookies."

Since this decision, President Carter has appointed Anne P. Jones, thereby creating a new majority on the commission, comprising members who have already shown that they are not averse to a departure from the traditional support of the status quo. The arrival of the new commissioners, coupled with the clear direction from the U.S. court of appeals in the WESH-TV case, may well presage a policy of honest and thorough consideration of license renewals.

The new voices on the commission are being heard on other issues as well. In the fall of 1978 the FCC undertook a new investigation, examining network practices for the first time in twenty years. The last such investigation produced the Barrow Report in 1958. The new inquiry is in response to the petition of the Westinghouse stations, and was announced by the FCC with the following: "Where some 50 percent of the programming aired by affiliates came from the networks in 1960, the amount is now two-thirds. And over the same period, network profits rose from $33.6 million to $208 million." With a new majority on the FCC it is possible that the investigation may bring about serious regulation.

The first demand for an investigation by Congress of the monopoly practices of the three networks was made in the Senate on May 13, 1954. Ohio senator John Bricker, who had run for Vice-President as the "conservative balance" to Thomas E. Dewey against the Roosevelt-Truman ticket, proposed to investigate what he called the "dictatorial practices of the networks," in connection with the introduction of a bill to require network regulation by the FCC.

Bricker's concern was occasioned by the fact that a group of prosperous central Ohio businessmen who were personal friends as well as constituents had recently raised and lost over a million dollars in a UHF venture in Dayton. Like many people who applied for UHF licenses in the early 1950s, they were under the impression that this was a good way to cash in on what they saw as a TV bonanza. Bricker's cronies spent a great deal of money putting a UHF television station on the air and then found that they could not get network affiliation. The networks had already arranged for their Dayton affiliations. The enterprise went broke, as did many another UHF venture.

In a speech introducing his bill, Senator Bricker said that "the ability of an individual station to obtain network programming too often determines whether that station lives or dies." He pointed out that during 1953 seventy-two construction permits granted by the FCC to provide for new television stations had been dropped, and that sixty of these were UHF allocations. He added that they had failed because "they were denied programs by the three networks."

The senator got his investigation, though his time in the limelight was brief. The following November the Democrats regained control of Congress, and Senator Warren Magnuson of Washington took over the chairmanship of the Commerce Committee, a body that has been examining network practices off and on ever since. But early in 1955 a report of Bricker's investigation was published under the signature of Harry Plotkin, the brilliant communications lawyer who had been minority counsel and succeeded to the majority post.

Plotkin regarded as unnecessary Bricker's proposal that the FCC be given power to regulate networks. (Although it is true that the commission has jurisdiction only over stations, it reaches the networks through the owned-and-operated licensees and also by its right to order the affiliates to take action or to refrain from taking action during network time). His most important recommendation was that there be a limitation on the amount of programming that an affiliated station could take from a network during specified times of each day. Plotkin restricted this proposal to affiliates in cities where there was no independent station, but as a practical matter this would have provided a most effective access rule even in the fifteen markets with independent stations, because no network could afford to program for so few outlets.

The House of Representatives first got into the act with an investigation of network practices conducted by the Antitrust Subcommittee of its Committee on the Judiciary. Then there was a congressional Oversight Committee inquiry into how the FCC was coping with the pressures brought to bear on them by network and other broadcasting lobbyists. This was followed by Senator Dodd's juvenile delinquency investigation, which led to attacks on television's portrayal of violence. Another House committee examined the effect of the networks' monopolization of prime time on small businessmen and recommended reforms that would afford local advertisers access to their potential customers. As we have noted, various congressional groups investigated the rating services, the quiz scandals, and alleged bias in network news.

Because every branch of the television industry must do business with the networks, congressmen who were investigating the monopoly encountered more than a fair share of recalcitrant witnesses. Some of the most recalcitrant were the operators of network-affiliated television stations. During one of the many hearings conducted by the Senate Commerce Committee's Subcommittee on Communications, on a day set aside for executives of the affiliated stations, Chairman John Pastore, increasingly annoyed at the parade of sycophantic apple-polishers, interrupted the proceedings to say, "I would like to make an announcement now. If there is any broadcasting station in the United States of America that is dissatisfied by the way they are being treated by CBS, NBC, or ABC, please let them come forward." None did.

Nor have program producers been eager witnesses. Roscoe Barrow opened his network investigation in 1956 by asking for comments from the producers. Believing that there was both anonymity and safety in numbers, a group of five companies formed an organization known as the Association of Television Film Distributors for the purpose of preparing and filing a memorandum with the Barrow committee. The association presented an outspoken document, carefully detailing what its authors considered the most flagrant network abuses. They proposed that the networks be divorced from program production, that time options be abolished, that networks be divorced from the syndication business and prohibited from demanding profit participations, and that they not be permitted to program all of prime time.

The only one of the five member companies that is still in business is the Columbia Pictures television subsidiary, then known as Screen Gems. Although the memorandum was a joint effort, Screen Gems president Ralph Cohen had written the final draft and supplied much of the relevant information. It was natural, therefore, that he was the one to be called as a witness some months later by crusty old Representative Emanuel Celler, chairman of the Antitrust Subcommittee of the House Committee on the Judiciary, which was investigating the networks' monopolistic practices.

The Cohen testimony was an embarrassing fiasco. He backed away from the strong position he had taken in the Barrow memorandum. Chairman Celler was moved to comment, "You were not so tender in your statement." He suggested that "in the interval something has happened to cause you to soften your attitude."

"Nothing has happened," Cohen answered. The reply was, to put it charitably, inaccurate. During the period between the composition of the memorandum and the hearing, Screen Gems had sold a number of series to the various networks.

That was the end of the Association of Television Film Distributors. From that time forward, the program producers who appeared before the various committees and boards of inquiry testified as though they were presidents of networks. During the protracted hearings of the FCC network study group, witness after witness testified that the producer yielded the profit participation voluntarily if not gleefully, that even where the network did not finance a pilot film they took some other sort of risk, and that there was a good and sufficient reason for every exaction to which they were subjected.

Inasmuch as the FCC is an administrative arm of the Congress, representatives and senators have generally let the commission do the legislating. As we have seen, they are constantly advising the commissioners and occasionally scolding them, but for the most part they have restricted their activities to holding hearings and making speeches and "recommendations."

In March 1977, however, Representative Lionel Van Deerlin of California, chairman of the House Communications Subcommittee and a former television newscaster, announced that his committee would embark on an investigation that would lead to a drastic revision of the Communications Act of 1934, the statute under which the television industry has functioned since it inception. Van Deerlin pointed out that the law antedated not only television, but also "coaxial cable, satellites, direct microwave beams, laser beams, fiber optics and a host of other technologies which may change the lives of Americans as sweepingly as the Industrial Revolution." He proposed that the law be rewritten "from basement to attic."

The suggestion of radical changes quite naturally upset the industry establishment. Technological progress and change in the art of communication over the last forty years did not make the existing law obsolete, according to industry spokesmen. On the contrary, they said, the Communications Act of 1934 is similar to the Constitution of the United States in that with continuing judicial and administrative interpretation it has been adapted to the changing times. CBS vice-president Bill Leonard said that under the 1934 act the American system of communications had become "the best on the face of the earth. . . . We produce entertainment in mind-boggling volume and sometimes even of high quality." He expressed concern that "in some sort of mad race to abolish it or reform it, or whatever, we not fritter away those precious rights for which we have fought so hard for so long." He of course added a reference to the First Amendment. In an official memo the National Association of Broadcasters asked: "Why is the public faced with any proposal or drastic restructuring of the broadcasting service it enjoys and relies on?" Despite the protests, the Van Deerlin committee went about its business. By the end of April 1977, the committee's staff had prepared 850 pages of background material which raised dozens of important questions, including, "If most viewers are satisfied with stations as conduits for national programming and if local programs fare poorly, should localism continue to be promoted?" "Should all television service be UHF?" "Should networks be required to give up their owned-and-operated stations?" and "Should competing applications be decided by a lottery or at an auction?"

On June 7, 1978, the Van Deerlin "rewrite," as it was called, was unveiled. The finished product, which had been twenty months in the making and was 217 pages long, fell far short of the promised "basement to attic" revision. It did not suggest an all-UHF service, an end to localism, a ban on network ownership of stations, or any of the other revolutionary reforms that its staff reports had indicated were under consideration. But there were some interesting provisions.

First, as we have already noted, the new law would solve the problem of funding public television by requiring payment of an annual license fee by each commercial user of the television spectrum. Most of the money from this source would become the sole source of government support for a new entity to be known as the Public Telecommunications Programming Endowment. The rest of the money would go to pay the bills of the Communications Regulatory Commission (the new name for an FCC with duties and budget cut back by 25 percent) and to encourage minority ownership in broadcasting and the expansion of telecommunications services to rural areas. It was Van Deerlin's guess that the license fee would bring in from $350 to 400 million per year.

The "rewrite" contained other new provisions. It would reduce the number of television stations a single entity can own from seven to five, of which not more than three could be in the fifty largest markets. Also, in the future a single owner could not own both radio and television stations in the same city (present owners would not be affected).

Under the new proposal, the Fairness Doctrine would continue to the extent that when controversial topics were covered, there would be the requirement of a right to reply, but there would be no requirement that a licensee editorialize at all. The industry would have to continue to adhere to the equal-time law, except that it would no longer apply to candidates for President, Vice-President, governor, or U.S. senator, or any other office requiring a statewide ballot. There would be no further federal regulation of cable TV; such regulation would be left entirely to the states.

Van Deerlin and his committee were disillusioned with the old process of license-renewal hearings based on the vague "public interest, convenience, and necessity" test, so they proposed that new licenses and existing franchises that become available shall be allocated at random among qualified applicants. The licenses would be extended from three to five years, but ten years after passage of the new law, licenses would be granted in perpetuity, subject only to challenge on the basis of improper operation. This, of course, meant abolition of the "public interest, convenience, and necessity" standard. Nothing in the entire proposal raised such a storm of protest as the suggestion that there be no such test, whereupon Van Deerlin announced that he would reconsider the inclusion of the old standard in a redraft of the legislation.

Further embarrassment was in store for the chairman when his staff members published their suggestion of the annual fees to be paid by each station to make up the $400 million needed to support public television and for the other ancillary purposes. The staff proposed that in New York City each of the six VHF stations pay a fee of $7 million, whereas the UHF stations were to pay only nominal amounts. The three New York independents protested, pointing out that $7 million for each of them was close to, if not more than, their annual profit; the network-owned-and-operated stations remained silent. The difference in profitability between affiliates and nonnetwork stations is, of course, so elementary in any consideration of the television business that Van Deerlin was forced to order the staff back to the drawing board. He announced that his "re-write" would be presented to the next Congress.

As soon as Van Deerlin had folded his tent, Senator Ernst F. Hollings, chairman of the prototype committee in the Senate, announced that he would also undertake an investigation of the Communications Act of 1934. He made it clear, however, that he did not believe that the law should be rewritten; on the contrary, he saw the problem as one of minor cosmetic sur-gery. Some observers viewed the Hollings announcement as a political reaction to the House committee rewrite, perhaps stimulated by broadcasters who believe that the joy of auto-matic renewal is outweighed by the pain of paying license fees. And while the form and substance of any congressional legisla-tion is uncertain, continued debate and public discussion are assured. For the first time since the advent of television there is a concerted attempt in at least one house to cure some abuses and correct some inequities that have long been the subject of investigation and conversation.

As we have pointed out, the basis for any legal action against monopoly and other destruction of what is known as "fair competition" is the antitrust laws—a body of legislations that includes the Sherman law, passed in 1890, the more com-prehensive Clayton act, enacted 24 years later, and the various amendments that have accrued over the years. These laws pro-hibit private business from engaging in various activities, some of which—such as competitors joining to fix prices or limit pro-duction—will not concern us here. The laws that speak to the network situation include those violations covered in the broad concept of "restraining trade," curtailing competition, and using unfair methods of competition.

Most prominent among those who produce and distribute films for television are the seven major motion-picture companies—Paramount, MGM, Twentieth Century-Fox, Warner Brothers, Universal, Columbia, and United Artists. These companies were defendants in a long antitrust action brought by the Department of Justice, a suit which culminated just as television began to assume its place in the American living room. The Supreme Court decided the case (*United States* v. *Paramount Pictures, Inc.*) in 1948, declaring the defendants in violation of the antitrust laws because of their dual operations as picture producers and owners or controllers of large chains of theaters that exhibited the films they had made. Producer and exhibitor were, in effect, the same body, and this had resulted in the fixing of admission prices, block booking (requiring an exhibitor to take pictures he didn't want in order to get the ones he did want), unfair discrimination against independent theater owners—a vertical monopoly in restraint of trade. As a result of this decision, the motion-picture companies spent the next few years working out a "consent decree," under which they had to divest themselves of ownership or control of theaters and of any direct connection with groups or pools of exhibitors; in short, they had to separate the production and the exhibition businesses. When these same companies found themselves dealing with the networks in the television business, it appeared to them that there was one standard for picture makers and another for networks. The networks not only controlled practically all of the exhibitors—that is, the television stations—they controlled the production as well. They furnished the shows in a manner similar to that which had been developed by the picture companies. The film men soon realized that network bargaining power dwarfed the privileges they had enjoyed prior to the Paramount case, and their immediate reaction was to go to the Department of Justice for relief. Their position was supported by Victor R. Hansen, then assistant attorney general in charge of the Antitrust Division, who testified before the Celler committee that "There is a striking similarity between the television industry structure and that movie pattern condemned in *Paramount* [*U.S.* v. *Paramount Pictures, Inc.*] . . . networks' control over the nation's TV stations dwarfs the movie makers' power over theaters condemned in *Paramount.*"

But the Department of Justice did not act upon the producers' grievance. At various times, individual companies planned to bring civil antitrust suits on their own, but they invariably retreated in fear of the consequences of suing their customers. It was not until 1967, when ABC and CBS announced that they were about to become part of the motion-picture industry, that is, when they were about to commence the production of major feature movies primarily for use in theaters, that a group of six companies brought suit.

The major motion-picture companies were outraged by the action of the two networks. All of them had television production and distribution subsidiaries that had been reasonably successful, but in each case the television business represented a relatively small portion of their earnings. Although exasperated by the effect of network monopoly practices on their television branches, these companies had played the game and submitted as gracefully as possible. However, when the network giants stepped into the theatrical moving-picture business, the alarms sounded in every top office in the industry. This was considerably bigger game. One theatrical motion picture can gross in one year as much as a subsidiary's entire television business can gross in the same period, and nobody knows how many good pictures can be made in a year.

The picture companies' complaint was grounded in fact. Ever since 1961 the networks had themselves become major buyers of theatrical movies. By 1967, movies accounted for 15 percent of network prime time, and even greater use was contemplated for the future. The motion-picture companies feared that as producers the networks might sell to themselves or at least use their own productions as a weapon to drive the market price down, or perhaps a combination of both. This would prove most damaging to the movie companies because the income from posttheatrical sale of a picture to a network, supplemented by later syndication, was often necessary for the picture's financial success.

Six of the seven major motion-picture companies (Warner Brothers, Paramount, Universal, United Artist, Columbia, and MGM) joined together and brought a civil antitrust lawsuit against CBS and ABC. NBC was not involved, because it had not gone into the theatrical production business. The seventh major producer, Twentieth Century-Fox, did not join in the action, presumably because it owned a television station in Minneapolis affiliated with the ABC network.

In their briefs the picture producers concentrated their attack on the networks' entry into picture production, which, they said, was part of a scheme to destroy the free market for the television licensing of movies—a plan that appeared to be succeeding, for although network profits had increased 230 percent in three years, rising from $50.1 million in 1970 to $184.8 million in 1973, the prices networks paid for theatrical feature films had remained the same.

CBS and ABC made about forty movies each, and then they

stopped. By 1975 their studios were dark. The picture producers' lawsuit may have had something to do with their closing
down, but a more likely answer is to be found in their balance
sheets. Both networks lost substantial amounts of money in
these ventures. They discovered that they had to carry their
own production losses, that in dealing with movie distributors
or theaters they were in a competitive business rather than a
monopoly, and that there is no captive audience, no ready-
made public that will watch the least objectionable picture no
matter what it is.

Meanwhile, the Department of Justice did nothing. Assistant Attorney General Hansen and others who headed the
Antitrust Division—Barnes, Turner, and MacLaren, for instance—expressed themselves before committees and in letters
to the FCC in language that left no doubt about the networks'
continuous violation of the Sherman Anti-Trust Act. But there
was no action until a suit was brought against NBC, CBS, and
ABC in 1973, ostensibly to prevent practices that had already
been stopped by the FCC. It was a peculiarly mild lawsuit,
one which Paul Laskin in *The Nation* on June 14, 1975, called
"shadow-boxing with the networks."

"Perhaps the most significant feature of the current suit,"
Laskin wrote, "is what it does not do. The fundamental institu-
tional structure of network TV broadcasting is to remain in-
tact. The suit accepts and does not challenge the relationship
that has grown up over the years between the networks and
their affiliates, although that relationship lies at the heart of the
networks' control of TV broadcasting."

On November 17, 1976, the Justice Department announced
that it had entered into a settlement with NBC and was negoti-
ating with the other two chains. NBC agreed that it would not
continue to do what it hadn't been permitted to do since 1971

and so was no longer doing anyway! In other words, the issues of exaction of a profit percentage and syndication of programs were academic; the rest of the discussion centered around the amount of programming that the network might own. The government was ready to allow ownership of two and a half hours of prime time and eight hours of daytime shows each week, and since NBC owned only one hour in prime time and nothing in daytime, there wasn't much to talk about. Two days later in the *New York Times*, Les Brown used the word *ludicrous* in discussing the settlement, saying, "If anything, NBC stands to gain from the settlement agreement in being freed from the courts and in saving prodigious legal fees that could run to hundreds of thousands of dollars."

The settlement contained a number of provisions that do not go into effect unless ABC and CBS also choose to adopt them. One such provision would prohibit NBC from obtaining exclusive yearly options on a series for longer than four years plus a one-year extension if the contract is renegotiated. This provision, among others, was bitterly criticized. A group of independent program producers said it was worse than useless in that it "legitimatizes past illegal practices and provides a vehicle for preserving an industry-wide anticompetitive code of behavior."

It is hard to understand why the labors of the mountain in this case brought forth so pusillanimous a mouse. Judge Robert Kelleher of the federal district court in Los Angeles, who approved NBC's consent judgment, said that the actions that the Department of Justice brought against the three networks "never were intended to break up their oligopolistic control of the television industry. . . . The proposed judgment must be viewed in the light of the government's limited objectives . . . merely to limit the exercise of that power."

When the Justice Department started this minor skirmish against the networks the attorneys for the motion-picture companies agreed to let their suit sit on a side track pending resolution of the department's case. It may sit there indefinitely, since the withdrawal of CBS and ABC from the movie business removed any impetus for litigation.

The apparent pointlessness of this suit ought not frustrate a more relevant use of legal processes. Federal courts enjoy wide discretion when it comes to directing remedies in antitrust actions. It is conceivable that a thorough and intelligent prosecution might lead to deintermixture or even an all-UHF system. Antitrust cases are notoriously slow-moving, sometimes taking a decade to reach a conclusion. Such a long process might cushion the shock to the mighty corporations whose interests would be attacked by such action. Unlike congressional debate, which often leads nowhere, once legal actions are undertaken they inevitably grind to a conclusion. It is certainly possible that someday there may be meaningful action on the antitrust front.

12

Which Way: Gadgetry or Government?

"We become what we behold."
—William Blake

There are those who tell us to forget trying to reform television; we will be saved by a proliferation of gadgetry, which they call technological developments. They beguile us with prophecies of fantastic new in-home services and devices that will bring entertainment from symphony concerts to pornographic movies at the drop of a five-dollar bill. But the perfection of new technologies usually takes longer than expected and often doesn't happen at all—and even when it does happen, it sometimes serves no useful purpose.

It is worth remembering that more than thirty years before its general acceptance, FM radio was uniformly acknowledged to project a better signal than standard radio. Ten years ago cable enthusiasts predicted that within the decade 80 to 90 percent of American urban homes would be wired for it, but there are still no signs of that happening. In 1969 we were assured that a simple taping device would be in almost every television home within a few years, but the manufacturers are still unable to market this machine at a price that the average viewer can afford. In 1972 we were informed that a simple and cheap plastic-disc recorder was about to flood the market, but the manufacturers still can't get its cost down to a popular range. Certainly the networks, although tinkering with gadgets, aren't worried about being replaced; during July 1978 CBS announced its purchase of the right to run the movie *Gone With the Wind* for twenty years at a price of $35 million, and NBC committed $21.5 million to license *The Sound of Music* for twenty-two years.

More significantly, however, the gadgetry doesn't change television programming or the economic operations that have made it what it is. Cable TV with all its channels brings old TV and theatrical movies into the home, and adds services like stock-market reports and comparison-shopping reports, and may even allow a viewer to call back to the transmitting source or to the retail store or perhaps to the local police or fire department—but this has little to do with the basic problem.

It has been pointed out that transmission by means of satellite could create a multiplicity of television channels, and indeed it could were there direct broadcast from satellite to home. But such transmission, if feasible, would not only destroy the networks, it would do away with the necessity for any television stations. That is why satellites will continue to be used simply to transmit programming from network to affiliates or from station to station—and to send pay movies and certain sports events to cable systems. These activities in no way affect or change television programming or the economic system that supports it.

Thus we come full circle, back to where we started: Why be concerned about the development of exotic new gadgetry when we already have at hand the technology to solve our problems—namely, UHF? There is little more promised by all of the new inventions than could be obtained by simply making the United States an all-UHF nation. The problem is not technological; it is political.

Because television can exist only by reason of the sufferance of the people in allowing the use of their airwaves for a profit-making purpose, one might assume that the people might achieve a better system by demanding it. Unfortunately, the organization of a complex industry has carried us beyond that point. Whenever the FCC considers changes in the industrial structure, it is besieged by the various pressure groups within the business. Regardless of whether it is networks, associations of affiliated stations, independent stations, major-network producers, syndicators, or cable owners, each group bases its argument on "the public interest," which coincidentally is always identical with its own profit interest. There are often citizen groups that bring their views on these same questions to the attention of the commissioners—organizations such as Action for Children's Television, the Boston-based consumer group that is interested in increasing and improving children's programming, and the Office of Communication of the United Church of Christ, which together with the National Citizens Committee for Broadcasting has also been asking for programming improvement. These people have no financial ax to grind, which diminishes rather than enhances their power, since there is a sort of implied assumption that it is the duty of the FCC to referee (if it cannot reconcile) the profit interests of the various branches of the industry.

There are examples in American history of important national reforms that were instigated and made possible by mass organizations of citizens such as the Abolitionists, Prohibitionists, the civil rights groups led by Dr. Martin Luther King, Jr., and the opponents of the Vietnam war. But it is doubtful that any such mass movement, however inspired, can radically alter television programming or practices, simply because we labor under the impression that we vote for or against a television show by turning the dial. Of course we now know that the choices television offers are artificially limited, and that the viewer makes the least objectionable of the choices he has at the moment. But as meretricious as those choices may be, we seem to be unable to give up the belief that the Nielsen rating truly records the voice of the people.

Even though a mass movement may never materialize, smaller groups of alert citizens can generate change. We have taken note of the awakened sensitivity to television's problems shown by the Communications Subcommittee of the House of Representatives and its staff in connection with the "rewrite" of the Communications Act, as well as the new majority of the FCC, which, in turn, indicates that the Executive Department of the government is aware of what goes on in the television business. Despite these signs, however, a healthy cynicism is justified when dealing with television in the political area. We are reminded of the many years of almost continuous congressional investigation and the previous network "studies" by the FCC. That these inquiries produced volumes of testimony and no action other than the Prime-Time Access Rule may well be because politicians recognize that the networks' control of televised news is unquestioned. The power of this medium to influence voters is known to all elected officials, but most clearly to those at the top.

The late Paul Porter, who had been a prominent Washington lawyer and a member of the FCC, told me the following story about his partner, Thurman Arnold. Long before television, while Franklin D. Roosevelt was president, Thurman Arnold served as assistant attorney general in charge of the Antitrust Division. Arnold and his associates had spent months preparing an antitrust complaint against a number of prominent motion-picture companies. A press conference had been arranged for the day on which the lawsuit was to be filed. Arnold was about to make what would certainly be a newsworthy announcement, when word came from Francis Biddle, the attorney general, to hold things up. Biddle had received an emergency call from the White House, directing him to see the President immediately. A few moments later, Biddle called Arnold on the phone.

"Call it off," he said, "we're not filing the suit."

The action was never filed. Nor was an official reason ever given to Arnold. But according to Porter, Arnold later found out that Roosevelt had been afraid that the picture companies would retaliate in their newsreels, and he was worried about the effect on him and his administration in the forthcoming national elections.

In those days, five-minute newsreels were used as curtain-raisers before the main feature picture in movie houses. They might indeed have been manipulated for political purposes. But the number of people who saw those films in theaters once a week is only a small fraction of those who now watch television news at least once a day in their living rooms. I would not think that today's statesmen are any less astute politically than was President Roosevelt.

Roosevelt was the last President who could constitutionally run for reelection more than once. During a second term, therefore, even a politically sensitive President can now feel free to push his attorney general to move for the substitution of an all-UHF television system or any other method that would break up the network monopoly. The decision in any such case will be made by judges who never face election. It is probably true that our courts are the least democratic branch of our government, but it is they who are often the people's only protection against the power of organized wealth and propaganda.

Although men have argued throughout the ages about private ownership of land and the minerals beneath it, and occasionally even about ownership of rivers and lakes, there has never been any question about ownership of the air. The channels of communication through the air belong to everybody. The American people have given the right to use these channels, gratis, to private interests, who in turn have used them to amass profits hitherto unmatched in our land. Those same interests also use the rights as a medium of propaganda to perpetuate the people's prodigality. In some circles, this might be called a con game. It has gone on for over thirty years. But can you really fool all of the people all of the time?

As television programming continues to deteriorate, public resentment will rise. When the people are fully conscious of an evil, their government—whether on the executive, legislative, or judicial level—can be forced into action. It can happen, aided by our constant vigilance and prodding.

INDEX

ABC, 8–9, 81, 127
   affiliates of, 27, 187
   antitrust cases against, 76,
      186–90
   News, 90–91, 92, 102
   Nixon interviews and, 91, 92
   owned and operated stations, 43,
      48
   profits, 10
   rise of, in ratings, 144
   "Soap" and, 117–19
   See also networks, commercial
Action for Children's Television,
   193
advertisers, 4–6, 42–45, 48, 60,
   105, 140
   programming controlled by,
      xvi–xvii, 5–6, 29, 44, 60, 67,
      68–70, 83, 86, 129–31
   public television and, 158, 159
   ratings and size of audience, 6,
      140
   small businesses and local, 178
   UHF stations and, 27
   violence and sex on television
      and, 117, 119
advertising, 13, 59–64, 129
   affiliated stations' income from,
      59–64, 183
   cigarette, 57, 154
   cost of commercial time, 10,
      48–49, 140
   cost-per-viewer rates, 48, 61, 78,
      140

income to networks from, x, 10,
   59–64
independent stations' revenue
   from, 48, 49
number of commercial minutes
   available, 63–64
price of advertised item and,
   153–54
sale of 30- to 60-second
   announcements, 60
spot, 122–24, 129
advertising agencies, 6, 7, 9, 44, 48,
   61, 71, 83, 90, 123
affiliated stations, 5, 26, 27, 29, 42,
   43–66 *passim*, 121, 139–40,
   141–42, 145, 178–79, 187
   accountability of, to FCC, 64–65,
      177–78
   income from advertising to, 59–64,
      183
   lack of control over programming,
      64–66
   network's economic hold on,
      47–48, 49, 52, 65
   reruns shown by, 35
   spot advertising by, 122–24
   with UHF frequencies, 27, 28
Agnew, Spiro, 93, 100
"All in the Family," 78, 115, 126
American Broadcasting Company.
   See ABC
American Civil Liberties Union,
   118
American Federation of Radio
   Artists, 35

American Federation of Television and Radio Artists, 160
American Museum of Natural History, 131
American Rating Bureau service (Arbitron), 31
American Telephone and Telegraph Company, 44, 60
anchormen, 99, 100
Arbitron. *See* American Rating Bureau service
Arlen, Michael, 12, 98, 102–3
Arnold, Thurman, 195
Association of Independent Television Stations, 79
Association of Television Film Producers, 179–80
Atlantic, The, 102
Aubrey, James, 88–89
audience flow, 6–7, 8, 140

Baker, Russell, 13
Bakersfield, California, 27
Baltimore, Maryland, 23, 28
"Baretta," 113
Barrow, Roscoe L., 165, 176, 179
barter network, 29
B.B.D.&O., 71
Beebe, Dr. Jack H., 7, 141, 169
Bernstein, Carl, 101
"Beverly Hillbillies," 9
Biddle, Francis, 195
Blank, David, 10
"Blue Book," 146, 162
"Blue Light," 81
Boggs, Sen. Hale, 88
Boston Herald-Traveler, 58
boycott threats, 118–19
bribery, ix–x, 38–39, 68
Bricker, John, 121, 176–77
Brinkley, David, 97, 98

Brinkley, Dr., 116
Bristol-Myers Company, 129
British Broadcasting Corporation, 160
British-produced programs, 159, 160–61
Broadcasting, 78
Brown, Les, 4–5, 9, 189
Bryant, Ashbrook, 165
Burch, Dean, 167, 169
Burger, Justice Warren, 172

cable television, 148–52, 155–56, 191, 192
Califano, Joseph, 102
Capital Cities, 136
Carter, President Jimmy, 99, 175–76
CBS, 9, 11–12, 57, 78, 80–81, 113, 192
  affiliates of, 27, 63–64
  antitrust cases against, 76, 186–90
  game show scandals, 69–70, 80–81
  News, 88–89, 90, 91, 92, 96, 98–99, 101, 102
  Nixon interviews and, 91, 92
  owned and operated stations, 43, 49
  UHF stations bought by, 25
  VHF argument with FCC, 20–21
  Viacom and, 126, 127
  winner-take-all tennis matches, 174–75
  See also networks, commercial
CBS "Saturday Night Movie," 64
channel 1, 21
channel 13 (New York City), 134–35

Celler, Emmanuel, 179–80, 186
censorship, 105–19
Channing, Carol, 40
character merchandising, 127–28
children, 56
    viewing habits of, xi, xii
Christian Life Commission of the
    Southern Baptist Convention,
    118
cigarette advertising, 57, 154
Cincinnati, Ohio, 23, 28
"Cisco Kid," 149–50
citizen groups, 118–19, 156,
    193–94
Clayton Anti-Trust Act, 184
Cohen, Jerry, 96
Cohen, Ralph, 179–80
color television, 20, 21
Colson, Charles, 102
Columbia Broadcasting System. See
    CBS
Columbia Pictures, 125, 179, 187
commercials. See advertising
Committee to Eliminate the UHF
    Handicap on Public Television,
    156
Communications Act of 1934, 19,
    112
    revision of, 161–62, 180–84, 194
Communications Regulatory
    Commission, 182
Community Antenna Television,
    148–49
competition, 167–68, 184
    among commercial networks,
    2–3, 10, 144
copyright law, 150, 151
Corinthian company, 136
Cousteau, Jacques, 90–91
Cowan, Lou, 70

Cowles Broadcasting Company,
    170–71
"C.P.O. Sharkey," 10
Cronkite, Walter, 102
Cushing, Archbishop Cardinal, 106

deintermixture plan, 136–37, 156,
    190
demographics, 8–9, 10, 80, 113
distributors, 37, 124–27
    See also producers of television
        programs; syndication
documentaries, 87, 89–91
    See also news, network; specials
Dodd, Thomas, 82–85, 178
Doerfer, John, 167
Dorso, Richard, 84–85
Dossee, Judge Robert, 110–11
Douglas, Mike, 46
Due to Circumstances Beyond Our
    Control (Friendly), 88

educational stations, 15, 157
elderly audience, 8–9, 156
Emerson, Faye, 106
Equal Time rule, 117, 183
ethnic and economic minorities,
    159

Fairness Doctrine, 95, 117, 182
family hour, 112–16, 117
FCC. See Federal Communications
    Commission
Federal Communications
    Commission (FCC), 18, 19, 43,
    45, 49, 50, 51, 62, 77, 111, 114,
    123–24, 128, 132, 164–76, 177,
    180, 182, 193
    attempts to help UHF stations,
        25, 27
    "Blue Book," 146, 162

Federal Communications (*Cont.*)
cable television and, 150
censorship of networks by, 106,
112, 115, 116–17
license renewals and challenges,
57–59, 95–96, 101, 104, 116,
164, 168–69, 170–76, 183
licensing of VHF band, 19–22,
138
local stations' responsibilities to,
64–65
members of, 166–67, 175–76
Network Study Committee, 6–7,
55, 70–72, 89, 139, 164–65
pay TV and, 155
policy of localism, 22–23,
138–39, 182
Prime-Time Access Rule. *See*
Prime-Time Access Rule
public television and, 156
UHF permits and, 20–22, 23,
137–38, 177
Federal Radio Commission, 19
Federson, Don, 8–9
Ferguson, Judge Warren J., 115
Ferris, Charles D., 31, 148
film, 37, 45–46, 144
50–50 plan, 139–40
"Firestone Hour," 5–6, 60
first-run shows
number of episodes per season,
14, 35, 36, 146–67
produced for syndication, 46,
53–54, 67–68, 85–86, 142–43
See also reruns; series; "strips"
Ford, President Gerald R., 151
Ford Foundation, 157
foreign sales, ix–x, 34, 36–37, 124,
125, 128, 131
See also syndication
Frankel, Art, 79

freedom of speech, 106–7, 111,
116, 117, 181
Friendly, Fred, 88–89, 98, 107
fringe time periods, 35
Frost, David, 91–92
FRS Associates, 7

gadgetry, 191–92
game shows, 54, 56
scandals of 1959, 69–70, 80–81,
178
General Tire Company, 42
Gerbner, George, xiii, 13–14,
107–9
Gleason, Jackie, 147
Gone With the Wind, 192
"Good Times," 78
government control of networks.
See censorship; Federal
Communications Commission;
U. S. Congress; U. S.
Department of Justice
Griffin, Merv, 46
Gross, Larry, xiii, 13–14, 107–9
Gulf and Western Corporation, 42
Gypsy Rose Lee, 36

Halberstam, David, 102
Haldeman, H. R., 91
Haley, Alex, 12
Hannie Calder, 64
Hansen, Victor H., 186, 188
Harris, Ellen Stern, 161
"Hawaii Five-O," 113
Hearst, William Randolph, 93
"Hee-Haw," 9
Hollings, Ernst, 184
Home Box Office, 152, 154
"Honeymooners, The," 147
Hoover, President Herbert, ix
Horowitz, Vladimir, 88

Hundred Million Dollar Lunch, The (Quinlan), 58

"I Love Lucy," 98
independent stations, xvi, 15, 27, 28, 29, 46, 48, 54, 55, 134–39, 144, 178, 183
Internal Revenue Service, 39
Ives, David, 161

Jankowski, Gene, 175
Johnson, President Lyndon B., 102, 103
Johnson, Nicholas, 111, 169
Jones, Anne P., 176
Journal of Communication, xiii
juvenile delinquency, 82–85, 106–7, 109–10, 178
J. Walter Thompson, 71

Kaiser Aluminum Company, 6, 7
"Kaiser Aluminum Hour," 6–7, 60
Kansas City, Missouri, 23, 28, 113
KCET (Los Angeles), 156–57
Kelleher, Judge Robert, 189
Kintner, Robert, 83–84, 85
Klein, Paul, 14–16, 147
KNXT (Los Angeles), 175
"Kojak," 109, 113
"Kraft Music Hall," 60
KTTV (Los Angeles), 54

Landis, Kennesaw Mountain, 2
Lane, Thomas L., 106
Langman, Anne, 78–79
Laskin, Paul, 188
"Lawrence Welk Show, The," 8–9
Lear, Norman, 81, 115, 126
Least Objectionable Program, Theory of, 15–17
Lee, Robert E., 167

Leonard, Bill, 181
Levathes, Peter, 6–7
Levy, Mark R., 100–101
license renewal and challenges, 57–59, 95–96, 101, 104, 116, 164, 168–69, 170–76, 183
licensing fees, 183, 184
Liggett & Myers Tobacco Company, 130
live broadcasting, 45–46, 96
"Live from Lincoln Center," 159
Los Angeles Times, 41
Lowe, Charles, 40
"Lucky Strike Hit Parade," 60
Lumbard, Judge J. Edward, 30
Lyons, James, 32–33

McCann-Erickson, 71
McConnaughy, George, 167
McDonald, Torbert, 168–69
McGannon, Don, 57, 63–64
McLuhan, Marshall, 13
Magnuson, Warren, 177
"Malibu Run," 83
"Man and the Challenge," 83–85
Manning, Dr. Willard G., Jr., 7, 141, 169
"Mannix," 113
"Mary Tyler Moore Show, The," 78
"Masterpiece Theatre," 159, 160, 161
"Maude," 78
"Mayberry R.F.D.," 9
men, programming geared to, 9
Mendès-France, Pierre, 93
Meredith Publishers, 136
Metromedia Producers, 126
MGM, 76, 125, 185, 187
miniseries, 75–76
Mintz, Morton, 96

Mobil Corporation, 161
"Mona McClusky," 130
monopoly, 1–2, 18–30, 105, 121,
184
Moore, Richard M., 54
movies, 63, 144, 155, 185, 187, 192
made-for-television, 75–76, 99,
129
network production of, 186–88,
190
for syndicated programming, 47,
54, 138
Murrow, Edward R., 96, 104

Nation, The, 78–79, 188
National Association of
Broadcasters, 63, 95, 96, 115,
181
National Council of Catholic
Bishops, 118
National Black Media Coalition,
156
National Broadcasting Company.
See NBC
National Citizens Committee for
Broadcasting, 193
National Council of Churches, 118
"National Geographic" series, 131
nature, or animal, shows, 56
NBC, 6–7, 57, 81, 83–84, 127, 192
affiliates of, 27
antitrust cases against, 49–52,
186–90
game show scandals, 69
News, 91, 92, 101–2
Nixon interviews and, 91, 92
owned and operated stations, 43,
49–52
profits, 10
UHF stations bought by, 25
See also networks, commercial

networks, commercial
advertising on. See advertisers;
advertising
competition among, 2–3, 10, 144
economic hold over affiliates,
47–48, 49, 52, 65
increasing the number of, 28–29,
35–36, 138, 141
making of the monopoly, 18–30
as natural monopoly, 2, 3
network-of-the-day plan, 141–42
news departments. See news,
network
option to renew series of, 77, 78,
80, 189
as producers, 76–77, 81, 166,
185–87, 190
producers and. See producers of
television programs
profits. See profits, network
program content controlled by,
79–85, 114–15
programming. See programming,
television
regulation of. See censorship;
Federal Communications
Commission; U. S. Congress;
U. S. Department of Justice
related businesses, entry into,
120–33, 165, 186–88, 190
self-censorship by, 115
spin-off rights of, 77–78, 128
See also ABC; CBS; NBC; and
specific related topics, e.g.,
affiliated stations; producers;
syndication
news, network, 87–104, 178
anchormen, 99, 100
difference between ordinary
news and, 97, 98

exclusion of independent
productions from, 89–92
government's power over, 101–2,
104
instant analysis by, 101
power of, 92–100, 103–4, 194
problem of selection of, 94–95,
96–99, 102–3
as profit maker, 87, 89, 97, 104
ratings and, 98–99, 104
survey of audience's reasons for
watching, 100–101
Vietnam War coverage by,
102–3
Watergate coverage by, 101–2
newspapers, 93, 94–95, 96
Newsweek, 114
New York Daily News, 58
New York magazine, 15, 147
New York Times, xv, 4, 13, 91, 96,
118, 189
Nielsen Company, A. C., 39–41
security of names of Nielsen
homes, 39–41
Nielsen ratings, 12, 31–32, 39–41,
69, 92, 99, 178
Nixon, President Richard M., 90,
91–92, 101
NTA, 127

O'Connor, John, 96
Oklahoma Publishing, 136
Omaha, Nebraska, 113
open-market economy, 1, 164
Opinion Research Corporation, 114
"Over Easy," 156
Owen, Dr. Bruce M., 7, 141, 161
owned and operated stations, 26,
27, 43, 48–52, 92, 104, 121–22,
124, 144–45, 175, 177, 182, 183
See also affiliated stations

Paley, William, 101
Panama Canal treaty, Carter's
speech on, 99
Paramount Pictures, 185, 187
Paramount Television, 79, 125
Parker, Everett C., 65–66
Pastore, John, 89, 114, 178–79
pay television, 148, 152–55, 192
Pentagon papers, 101
Philco Corporation, 50
Pierce, Franklin, 119
pilots, 73, 74–75, 79–80, 129–30,
180
plastic-disc recorders, 192
Plotkin, Harry, 177–78
"Poldark," 160
political candidates, equal-time rule
and, 183
Porter, Paul, 194–95
Post-Newsweek, 136
Power, Inc. (Mintz and Cohen), 96
President's Office of
Telecommunications Policy, 14
prime-time access period, 55–57
half-hour syndicated programs
for, 47, 54–56, 68, 85–86,
124, 126–27
Prime-Time Access Rule, 8, 47, 53,
55–57, 112, 124, 126–27, 128,
142, 144, 145, 165, 166, 167, 194
prime-time television, 53, 65–66,
138, 142, 178, 189
defined, xvii
family hour, 112–16, 117
number of commercial minutes
during, 63
prime-time access period. *See*
prime-time access period
reruns in, 146–47
sex and violence on. *See* sex on

prime-time television (*Cont.*)
television; violence on
television unsponsored
programming in, 145–46
producers of television programs,
29, 42, 62, 67–86, 140, 151,
179–80
advertiser-controlled
programming and. *See*
programming, advertiser-
controlled
antitrust action against the
networks by, 185–90
bribery and expensive gifts given
by, ix–x, 38–39, 68
British, 159, 160–61
deficit financing of programs by,
74–77, 78, 81
example of program's
development, 72–75
foreign sales, ix–x, 34, 36–37,
124, 125, 128, 131
network-controlled programming
and. *See* programming,
network-controlled
networks as, 76–77, 81, 166,
185–87, 190
networks' option to renew series,
77, 78, 80, 189
of news programs, 89–92
for pay TV, 153
prime-time access period and,
55–56, 124, 126–27
profits to, 37–38, 78, 128–33
passim, 145, 151, 165, 180
program content, degree of
control over, 79–85, 114–15
ratings and, 33–34, 38
reruns and, 35–38, 113–14,
124–27
of specials, 72, 131

spin-offs and, 77–78, 128
syndication and, 46–47, 52–54,
67–68, 85–86, 124–27, 128,
142–43, 144
See also program costs;
syndication
production costs. *See* program costs
Professor and the Commission, The
(Schwartz), 168
profits
to cable television, 151
to networks, xi, 10, 18, 45,
61–62, 78, 87, 89, 97, 104,
121, 128–33 *passim*, 145, 165,
176, 180, 187
to producers, 37–38, 78, 128–33
passim, 145, 151, 165, 180
to stations, 44
program costs, 10, 36, 38, 52, 60,
62, 132
program development, 72–75
See also pilots
programming, television, xi, xiii–xiv
advertiser-controlled, 5–6, 29,
44, 60, 67, 68–70, 71, 72, 83,
86, 129–31
demographics and, 8–9, 10, 80,
113
50-50 plan, 139–40
Least Objectionable Program
Theory, 15–16
network-controlled, 6–8, 26–27,
44, 53, 65–66, 69–85, 130,
139–40, 176, 185
of news. *See* news, network
public's taste and, 11–13
on public television, 156, 157,
159–61
quality, xvi–xvii, 5–6, 135, 156,
162
ratings and. *See* ratings

of UHF stations, 24, 27
of unsponsored material in prime
  time, 145–46
See also family hour; prime-time
  access period
promotional announcements, 64
public, consuming, 11–12, 13
Public Broadcasting Service (PBS),
  157–61
public service announcements, 63,
  64
Public Telecommunications
  Programming Endowment, 182
public television, 156–62, 182

Quello, James, 173
Quinlan, Sterling, 58
quiz shows. *See* game shows

"Race for Space," 89
radio, 3, 5–6, 19, 22, 35, 135, 138,
  167, 191
  sustaining programming on,
    145–46
Radio Commission, 116
rate card, 48, 140
ratings, 6, 8, 9, 31–41, 101, 140
  cost of commercial time and, 10,
    33
  investigations of, 39, 178
  network news and, 98–99, 104
  overnight, 144
  percentage of homes with sets in
    use during prime time, 14
  public television's, 156, 157
  producers and, 33–34, 38
  rigging of, 39–41
  of "Roots," 12
  share of audience, 33–34
  See also demographics; Nielsen
    ratings

RCA, VHF argument and, 20
regulation. *See* censorship; Federal
  Communications Commission;
  U. S. Congress; U. S. Department
  of Justice
religious groups, boycotts by,
  118–19
reruns, 14, 35–36, 37, 54, 113–14,
  138, 146–47
  See also strips
"Rhoda," 77–78
Rice, Michael, 159
Rich, Lee, 78
Rintels, David, 81
Rockefeller, John D., Sr., 2
"Rookies, The," 113
Roosevelt, President Franklin D.,
  195
"Roots," 12–13
Roots (Haley), 12
rural audiences, 9, 182

Sarnoff, David, 1, 12, 59, 99–100
satellite transmission, 192
"Scarlet Letter, The," 161
Schramm, Dr. Wilbur, 106–7
Schwartz, Bernard, 168
Screen Gems, 76, 179, 180
second season, 143–44
"See How She Runs," 99
"See It Now," 96
Selmur Productions, 81
series
  development of, 72–75
  option to renew, 77, 78, 80, 189
  producer's creative independence
    over a, 79–86, 114–15
  See also first-run shows; pilots
"Sesame Street," 156
sex on television, 83–85, 106, 107,
  112, 113, 115, 117–19

Sherman Anti-trust Act, 2, 51, 184, 188

Showtime, 152

Sinn, John L., 84

"Sixty-Four Thousand Dollar Challenge, The," 69–70

"Sixty-Four Thousand Dollar Question, The," 6–7, 69–70

Sound of Music, The, 192

Sparger, Rex, 39–41

special-interest groups, boycotts by, 118–19

specials, 72, 130–31, 144
    See also documentaries

spin-offs, 77–78, 128

sponsors. *See* advertisers

sports events, 9, 155, 174–75, 192

spot advertising, 122–24, 129

Standard Oil Company, 2

Stanton, Frank, 25, 89, 102
    reaction to quiz show scandals, 69–70, 80–81
    testimony before congressional committees, 11–12, 30, 42, 88, 121

stars, 62, 72, 128

"Starsky and Hutch," 114

State University of New York at Albany, 100

station-representative business, 122–24

Station Representatives' Association, 123

stations. *See* affiliated stations; independent stations; owned and operated stations; Ultra High Frequency (UHF) transmission and stations; Very High Frequency (VHF) transmission and stations

Steiner, Peter O., 163

stock of television networks, 10

Storer company, 136

"strips," 35–36, 37, 47, 54, 55, 113–14, 144
    See also reruns; syndication

Supreme Court, 49–52, 115–16, 151, 172

Susskind, David, 70–72

sustaining programming, 145–46

syndication, 9, 45, 52–54, 67–68, 128, 131, 142–43
    cable television and, 150–51
    networks' attempts to control, 124–27, 165
    of news documentaries, 90, 91–92
    prime-time access period and, 47, 54–56, 68, 85–86, 124, 126–27
    types of syndicated programming, 46–47
    See also foreign sales

talent agencies, 122, 146–47

Talent Associates, 70

talent unions, 54

talk shows, 54, 138

tape, 37, 45–46, 97, 144

taping devices, 191–92

Tarlton, Robert, 149

Taylor, Arthur, 112

teasers, 106

Television: The Business Behind the Box (Brown), 4–5, 9

Television Economics (Owen, et al.), 7, 141

television sets, 21, 23–24, 25

"Texaco Star Theater," 60

"Three's Company," 10

Time, Inc., 152

"Time of Man," 131

Toledo, Ohio, 28
"Tombstone Territory," 129–30
Tors, Ivan, 83
Transamerica Corporation, 42
Trenton, New Jersey, 21
trusts, 2
Tucson, Arizona, 28
TV Guide, 114
Twentieth Century-Fox, 76, 81, 125, 185, 187
"Twenty-One," 69

Ultra High Frequency (UHF) transmission and stations, 20–22, 23–27, 29, 46, 48, 136–39, 156, 177
all-UHF, system, 135–36, 182, 190, 193, 196
conditions beneficial to, 27–28
public television on, 156–57
Unger, Maurice, 85
United Artists, 83–84, 125, 126, 185, 187
United Church of Christ, Office of Communications of, 65, 118, 139, 193
United Methodist Church, 118
United States Catholic Conference, 118
U. S. Congress, 19, 30, 42, 55, 65, 88, 96, 106, 114, 164, 176–84, 194
Dodd Committee investigation, 81–85, 178
House of Representatives, 39, 54, 69, 81, 96, 145, 160–61, 174, 178, 180–84, 194
Senate, 11–12, 54, 69, 96, 98, 106–7, 128–29, 166, 176, 178–79, 184
UHF stations and, 25, 177

U. S. Defense Department, 89
U. S. Department of Justice, 51, 76, 120, 122, 124, 165, 185–90, 195
United States of America v. *American Broadcasting Companies, Inc.*, 120
United States of America v. *CBS, Inc.*, 120
U. S. Supreme Court. *See* Supreme Court
U. S. Surgeon General, 107
United States v. *Paramount Pictures*, 185, 186
Universal-MCA, 125
Universal Studios, 185, 187
University of Pennsylvania, Annenberg School of Communications, xiii
University of Southern California, School of Journalism of, 99–100
"Upstairs Downstairs," 160
urban audiences, 9, 109

Van Deerlin, Lionel, 161–62, 180–84
Very High Frequency (VHF) transmission and stations, 19–21, 24, 43, 135–36
FCC policy of localism and, 22–23, 138–39
independent, 27, 48, 49, 54, 136–37
public television on, 156–57
strength of signal of, 26
thirteen channels of, 19, 20, 21
Viacom, 127, 152
Vietnam War, news coverage of, 98, 102–3
View from Highway 1, The (Arlen), 12, 98

viewing habits, xi–xii, xiii, xvii, 14
  watching least objectionable
    program, 13–14, 15–17
  See also audience flow;
    demographics
violence on television, 81–85,
    106–12, 117
  defenders of, xii–xiii
  family hour and, 112–16
  juvenile delinquency and, 82–85,
    106–7, 109–10, 178
  violent crime and, xii, 109–10

Wallace, Mike, 91
Walters, Barbara, 92, 99
"Waltons, The," 78
Warner Brothers, 125, 185, 187
Warner Communications, 42
Watergate news coverage, 101–2
Welk, Lawrence, 8–9
Wenner, Jann S., 87, 99–100
WESH-TV (Daytona Beach, Fla.),
    170–72, 176
Westinghouse Corporation, 42,
    49–51, 52, 57, 62, 63–64, 136,
    176
WGBH (Boston), 159
WGBH (Boston) Educational
    Foundation, 161
WGN-TV (Chicago), 49

White, Associate Justice Byron R.,
    115–16
White, E. B., xv
White, Theodore, 90
Wiley, Richard, 111–12, 114, 115,
    116, 170–71
Wilkey, Judge Richard, 171–72
William Morris Agency, 122
Worldvision, 127
Wirth, Timothy, 107
WLBT-TV (Jackson, Miss.), 172
WNET (New York City), 158–59
WNEW (New York City), xv, xvi
Wolff, Sanford, 160–61
Wolper, David L., 89–90
women, programming geared to,
    ages 18 to 49, 8–9, 56, 140
Woodward, Bob, 101
WOR-TV (New York City), 49
WPIX-TV (New York City), 49,
    58–59, 172–73, 175
Writers Guild of America, 81
Wussler, Robert, 174–75

Xerox Corporation, 90
XEWT-TV (Tijuana, Mexico), 27

Young & Rubicam, 7, 129

Zamora, Ronney, 109–10
Ziv Company, 149–50